The Lies

The Truth &

The Blame

By

S. Hickman

Table of Contents

Introduction...1

Chapter 1 4

Chapter 2...9

Chapter 3...26

Chapter 4...58

Chapter 5...76

Chapter 6...84

Chapter 7...92

Chapter 8...100

Chapter 9...110

Introduction

'The truth will set you free. But not until it is finished with
you.'

– David Foster Wallace

Everybody always says that honesty is the best policy and to always tell the truth. I learned that telling the truth can bring its own pain and suffering; even if it does not belong to you. I learned that if you speak the truth, you can destroy families, unearth more than you ever thought was possible, and come out of it all as the one to blame. I don't know if I would change what I did, but I will always feel guilty and responsible for the fallout.

This is the story of my family, the secrets, the lies, and the discovery of the truth. Names have been changed to protect those involved, but all the events that happened are absolutely true.

I wrote this book hoping to reach people in similar situations and to help them with my story. I didn't always have help, and I have had to deal with so much on my own, which can be very dark. I hope my story shows that things get better and that you should always look out for number one.

I have only ever told this story to those closest to me, and although it has been cathartic to write about it, it has been hard reliving it all.

For the purposes of this book, I have referred to my father as 'He' or 'Him' because I physically struggle to call him dad.

Questions

*'If you live the questions, life will move
you into the answers'*

– Deepak Chopra

Do I wish I had never found it?

Do I wish I didn't know what I know now?

Should I have said anything?

Does counselling help?

Does everyone blame me?

How the hell have they forgiven Him?

How could they spend time with Him and not me?

Should I resent them for seeing Him?

Where would we all be now if I hadn't said anything?

Does this get easier?

Has it made me a different person, and would I be who I am today if it had never happened?

Is it better to run from it all and accept that everyone

blames me?

Am I that selfish person that they think I am?

So many questions constantly spiral around in my head.

Here are some of the answers and the story of my 38 years.

The most important question… Does it get better?

Chapter 1

'Broken relationships are a source of heavy heartbreak that seem to affect every family.'

– Jerry B Jenkins

So, where did it all begin?

I was living with my brother James and my parents in our family home. We were lucky to have such a beautiful home and have space to play and explore. The house was Edwardian. It had big, beautiful windows, high ceilings, and large rooms. It needed a huge amount of work, but it had so much potential. The house originally had four bedrooms, but previous owners extended it further to add two bedrooms. My family decided that we could split the house in two and create an annex for my grandparents to live in. We continued to live separate lives, but should anything happen; we would be just next door. We would get together for some Sunday lunches and special occasions, which was so nice.

My grandparents were amazing! My grandpa joined the military as soldier when he was just a boy. He falsified the date of birth on his birth certificate to enrol early because he absolutely knew that the military was where he belonged. It's all he wanted to do.

He had an amazing journey through the military, travelled the world, lived in Kenya, and was an amazing father and husband. During part of his career, he ran Junior

Leaders. This was an area of the military where the young soldiers came to be trained. My grandpa would get them fit and ready for the army, but he would also take the time to follow their careers throughout their military life to watch their progress. He always wanted people to succeed and prosper in whatever they chose to do. He was an amazing human being, and I miss him every day. He was the sort of person to restore faith in humanity.

My granny was a nurse in the military for a short time. She met my grandpa during her time in the army and believe it or not; they only knew each other for forty-eight hours before they were engaged to be married. They spent their lives together travelling the world and living in some amazing places. My granny gave up work when my grandpa was commissioned as an officer but continued to have a wonderful life with him by her side. He could never do enough for her. They truly were such a loving couple and were together until the end. I always thought it was the kind of loving relationship that I would want for myself.

'He' worked in finance when we first moved to the house. He earned good money as far as we were all aware and was able to provide his family with comfortable life, lovely holidays, Christmases, and Birthdays. All our family friends liked him very much. He was a good entertainer and a good host at parties. It all seemed like a happy, loving family. What more could we possibly want?

One of the best holidays we went on, and actually, the last one together was a trip to Canada. We travelled around British Columbia, Alberta, and all the way to Toronto. It was the most incredible place I have ever been. There was so much space, clean, fresh air, lakes, and mountains as far as you could see. There was amazing wildlife everywhere, from chipmunks to bears and moose. It was breath taking. I could absolutely see myself living somewhere like Canada when I was older.

My Mum worked with children with learning difficulties. Although she always taught, she decided to qualify to help with special needs children when my brother and I were both diagnosed as dyslexic. Mum helped us through our schooling and made sure that we left school with as many qualifications as possible. She really was a force to be reconned with, and we definitely had respect for her.

My brother James is two years older than me, and we had a reasonably good relationship. We would fight, as children do, but all in all, we got on pretty well. He struggled through school with his dyslexia and was very hard work as a child. My Mum had her hands full with my brother. For some reason, he was always seen as the 'golden child.' I think he knew how to schmooze the rest of my family and was very sociable, and of course, everyone thought he was amazing.

Then there's me. I have always thought I was different from the rest of my family. They have never really understood me or what I want from life. I am socially awkward and struggle in situations with strangers. I was bullied throughout school, which only made things more difficult for me. My family doesn't understand my need to talk about things, and if someone wrongs me, I will cut them from my life without question.

Well, by now, you must be wondering what I found.

I was around ten years old, and my brother James was about twelve. We were playing in the house as we normally would one weekend, we decided to play as very important businesspeople in the dining room. We decided to use His briefcase, which He took to work every day, as a prop. I remember the case perfectly. It was a deep red leather case with gold-coloured coded locks on the top. This particular day though, the case was unlocked.

James started taking paperwork out of the case, pretending he was doing some work when suddenly a magazine appeared with it. This magazine had images that we should not have seen at that age. Not only should we not have seen these images, but they were not what we would have expected. The pictures were of men!

My blood ran cold, my stomach was in my mouth, and I felt sick. I had goosebumps; I was shaking; my heart was beating out of my chest and the hairs on the back of my neck stood up. I started crying because I really didn't understand what was going on. James told me that it was 'one of those free ones they give out.' I didn't believe him. I don't know whether he was trying to protect me or whether he truly believed it. Strangely, he doesn't remember this, but I carried it with me, and I still do.

Sadly, from this point on, this made me very suspicious of Him. I remember Him going away on so-called business trips. I would get so upset as we all stood on our gravel driveway to say our goodbyes because I believed there was more to this than anyone else knew. Imagine having a secret like that at ten years old. Imagine looking at your dad in a whole different light after being such a daddy's girl. Imagine feeling like your tiny world was going to change in a huge way.

Chapter 2

'Suspicion is creative in its nature. It can bring out and develop the very evils it conceives.'

– John Daniel Barry

Do I wish I could have a simple life without drama, lies, and secrets? Of course, I do. But would I prefer knowing rather than living in that web of lies? Absolutely. But everything that came with it was heart breaking and life-changing.

He decided to quit his job in finance to become self-employed. This obviously gave Him a lot more freedom, and He was home alone a lot whilst Mum was at work. James and I were at school all day, so we were out of his way. He had absolute freedom, which would prove to be a disaster.

As I got older, my suspicions grew, and I continued to keep an eye on His behaviour. I would watch everything He would do. I would watch what He would look at when we would go into town; I would look at the internet history to see what He had been looking at. Unfortunately, I saw all the things I really did not want to see. All my trust in him was gone, and all I felt was anger.

On our trips into town, His gaze would wander to passing men on the street. It would make my skin crawl, and I would shake with anger and disgust. When I think about it now, it was just so blatantly obvious, and He had no desire to hide it, but He was completely unaware that I knew anything. I remember watching everything He would do to confirm my suspicions, and at every opportunity, He proved me right, which in turn, created more anger and pain.

When I started keeping an eye on His internet history, I found a lot more than I bargained for. There were chat rooms and websites where He was finding men to talk to and to meet with. This was really happening. I wanted it all to be a mistake and for me to have completely misread all the signs. He didn't know that I could look at his history and could see exactly what He had been looking at. It's amazing what you can teach yourself, even at a young age.

I then started to find a whole new side to Him. I found gambling sites and numerous credit card statements everywhere. This then created new suspicions and more worry. I couldn't bring myself to talk to my mum about anything because I knew how upset she would be, and I really didn't know at that point how much was really going on and how deep the rabbit hole went. It wasn't long until I found out just how bad the situation was.

After school, I went to an Equestrian college to do what I loved the most and studied horses for two years. It was amazing. I had to take a work placement as part of my course, and I had read about a western-style ranch down on Dartmoor with American and Canadian Quarter Horses. I got in touch with the owners, who were husband and wife, and they offered me the opportunity to go down there for three months to work with them. I would be roughing it in a caravan, but I didn't care. The idea of being out in the fresh air with such beautiful animals was all I could think about. I wouldn't be paid, but any tips were mine to keep.

My main job was to look after the horses and get them ready for all-day rides on Dartmoor for the guests who would stay at the ranch. I went along on the rides with the owner to get to know the routes and the horses, and soon I was able to take groups out on my own. We would ride half a day to a local pub that had a small paddock where we could tether the horses and have a pub lunch. We would then take them a different route home making up a whole day of riding.

There were some days when the fog would drop over the moors, and the visibility was horrendous. You could only just see your hand in front of your face, but no further. We taught the guests that horses will always find their way home. I had really fallen for one particular horse called Cody. He was a huge chestnut Quarter Horse and such a lovely boy. I showed the guests that I could literally drop the reins on Cody, and he would find his own way home without my help. We got back to the ranch safely every time, and it really taught the guests a lot about the horses. Such amazing animals.

Some evenings, I would go outside and lay on the hay bales in the fields and look at the stars. There was no light pollution there, so the clear night skies were so beautiful. It gave me even more of an appreciation for the world and nature. It was heaven and it completely opened my eyes up to what I wanted from life.

Sadly, time was up, and I had to leave this amazing place that I had fallen so in love with. Three months was just not enough. What an experience, and one that I will never forget and forever be grateful for because it brought me such peace.

That was the life; I could do it forever. Such a shame it was only short-term. The had been everything for me. The thought of going home was upsetting, and I would miss the calm of Dartmoor so much.

Years passed, and I continued to watch and take things in at home. It caused so much anger that as soon as I was old enough, I would go out with friends constantly, drinking too much to numb pain. This only made things worse, though. The alcohol would only exasperate any emotions I had, leaving me in tears at the end of every night. My friends would never find out the truth. To this day, I have only ever told my story to one person outside of my immediate family.

Before long, I was in a long-term relationship with a guy called Paul, who I had met through friends. I stayed at his family's house a lot to avoid being at home, and I wonder now if I had used the relationship as a way to get out of my situation. He was a nice enough guy, but he definitely had weaknesses in his personality, which meant his family took advantage of him a fair bit. We dated for about seven years in total.

Meanwhile, James had bought his own flat and was living about twenty minutes from home with his girlfriend. He was working a great job and doing really well for himself.

One day, I decided to go back to my house to collect some things. The study door was open, and He wasn't in there for once. This was a rare opportunity to see if I could find anything. I opened up the computer, and everything was unlocked. He must have just popped out quickly. I found numerous gambling shortcuts on the desktop screen and I started to really panic. Every time I would find things, my blood would boil. I was fed up with being the only one who knew about it all. I had enough of it, and I made up my mind to speak to my mum about things. But how?

I waited for an opportunity when He was out and my Mum had an evening in. I didn't know how and where to start. I only wanted to talk about the gambling, nothing else at this point. I didn't think I had the strength, and I had no idea how to break that sort of news to my own mother.

I told her that I had noticed some apps and shortcuts for gambling sites on the computer and that perhaps she should think about discussing it with Him. She looked instantly worried and looked close to tears. She didn't know the half of it. How would I ever tell her the rest? I couldn't tell her about the chat rooms or the meetings He was having. It was too much.

Mum told me that she would sit and have a chat with Him and would ask to see all the financials. I decided that this was a good time to get my stuff and head back to Paul's house. I never told him anything about it. I didn't think he had the maturity to deal with any of it, and I was terrified that he would tell other people. I really didn't want to be humiliated, and I really didn't want anyone to know. I was so embarrassed by the whole situation. I started to push him away a bit. I didn't want anyone getting close enough to find out my secrets.

I went to work as normal the following day. I had started working for an interior fit-out company as a Personal Assistant. I enjoyed it, but it wasn't really what I wanted to do.

I had a phone call from my mum when I was in the office. She was in tears and sounded like she was in a state of panic. I asked my boss if I could be excused for the rest of the day and drove back to the house to find out what had happened. That felt like the longest drive of my life. My adrenaline was pumping, my hands were shaking, and my jaw was chattering even though I wasn't cold. What had I done? Was this my fault?

When I got home, my mum, still in tears, said that He had run off after their conversation about money. He had admitted to being in a huge amount of debt which amounted to around £70,000. After He had admitted to it, Mum had told Him how disappointed she was and of course, in a fit of rage, told Him how pathetic He had been and how He had put the family in such an awful mess. She had told Him that he should be ashamed that His daughter had been tasked with breaking the news.

He had waited until she had gone to bed, took a box of painkillers from the medicine cupboard, and drove to the woods. He propped himself up against a tree and, one by one took all the tablets in the packet, followed by a bottle of alcohol.

There was a police officer at the house, and my brother had also arrived. My mum told us that He was missing, and so were some of the pills from the cupboard. James's first response was 'selfish prick.' Quite honestly, I felt the same. I didn't even cry. I just felt complete guilt. After all, I was the one to tell my mum all this news. The worst part was that I knew so much more, which could make it so much worse. Now was not the time to stoke the fire. I just felt sick, and it was more guilt than worry. Is that wrong?

The police had organized a helicopter and search dogs to go out and try to find him because it looked as if he was planning to end his life. I remember hoping that they wouldn't find Him because then the rest of His bullshit could remain a secret. I had grown to hate Him for all the things

He was putting my mum through. All the lies, cheating, and gambling. How much worse could it be? How could anyone live with themselves having so many secrets? I could never understand it.

Eventually, the helicopter found Him with a heat detector in the woods, and the dogs and officers followed. He was alive and was taken to a local hospital. We all went there to see Him. I felt nothing for Him except hate and embarrassment. I was wondering what the nurses and doctors must have thought. Did they think we had led Him to it? Or did they think He was the arsehole who would have left his family to avoid dealing with the problems? Afterall, that's what He had tried to do.

I could barely look at him, but all I remember was His pupils being abnormally large. He looked completely out of it. It was so awful to watch, and I still remember it like it was yesterday. I called Paul to inform him about the situation and where I was. I don't know what sort of response I was after, but his game of golf seemed to be a lot more important than my current shitty situation. I think this is the moment I realized that this relationship was not one of love but convenience and maybe just a friendship of sorts. He was clearly still not mature enough to be able to support me when I needed him. We had been together such a long time that it just felt familiar. On top of everything, was I really going to end our relationship? I felt numb and honestly could have just ended it on the phone, but that would have been wrong on my part.

When He was released and could come home, He was recommended to attend some counselling sessions to discuss any issues He may have and to make sure He wouldn't do it again. This made me feel a bit more positive, and I wondered if talking about things would help. Of course, He never went. That would mean confronting everything and admitting that He had done wrong. This only left the rest of us feeling like He didn't care enough to show us He was dealing with things and was willing to make changes.

My mum decided to stick by Him throughout, and unbelievably my poor Grandpa had to bail Him out. Grandpa paid off the £70,000 debt so that we wouldn't lose the house. Afterall it was their house too, so it was in their best interests. Unfortunately, that side of my family like to sweep things under the carpet and not actually confront anything, and He, like James, was always the golden child since he was young. Therefore, realistically there were no consequences for His behaviour. I concluded that He had taken the pills as a 'get out' and that He had no intention of ending His life. Funnily enough, this plan had worked for Him.

He had lost any kind of relationship with me now, not that the rest of my family could really understand that. They didn't know everything but knew enough to be at least a little angry, but no, it was all over and done with.

I did feel like I had missed an opportunity to talk to mum about everything He was up to, but how the hell do you tell someone that? I was going to have to keep it to myself but carrying something like that can really play with your emotions, and strangely I felt as guilty as He was for not saying anything.

In the coming weeks, I decided to move back to the house to make sure mum was ok and that things were settled. I also ended things with Paul as it just felt that the relationship had run its course. I was also still angry that my nightmare was put second to a game of golf. I guess situations like that really show peoples' true colours. I didn't feel sad about the break up. I think I was still numb to any kind of emotion other than anger and guilt. I actually felt relief that our relationship was over.

I left my job at the office and took a job working at a beautiful livery yard as an assistant manager, and after a year or so was allowed to move into an amazing flat on site. This was the best opportunity because it got me away from the constant stress and worry. It never leaves you, though. It was always in the back of my mind. What's He doing? Where's He going? Who's He spending time with? Is He gambling again? The biggest question for me though, was still, how has everyone so easily forgiven Him? I had to keep reminding myself that they didn't know what I knew.

I started seeing someone called Andy, who I had met online. He was in the RAF Regiment, and it felt like a strong relationship. He was a lot more mature and had military discipline. Of course, I hadn't told him anything about my family life and any of the secrets I was keeping. He lived about an hour away, but I would go and stay with him on some of my weekends off, and he would come to me. It worked in the short term and was a good distraction from the noise in my head.

I had been working at the yard for about three years and was really enjoying the work, the riding, and the beautiful horses we were entrusted with. The yard was on the most stunning estate with woodland, fields, and beautiful hacking. The outdoors was my happy place, and it gave me the space I needed to clear my head. The quiet and the nature around me were very healing. I had some great friends working with me, and life generally felt good. I was still in a relationship with Andy, which was going so well, and he was in the process of making the decision to leave the RAF and starting on the road to being a Personal Trainer.

I was working a weekend at the yard, which was always completely manic. We went to get one of the horses in from the field and prepare him for his owners' arrival. At this point, things became very hazy, but from what people have said, out of nowhere, the horse we were working on double-barrelled me with both back feet. He hit me in the side of the head and in my face, and threw me into a stable door.

The next thing I remember is waking up in the hospital with a doctor telling me that I had been in for three days. He told me that I had been kicked and had damage to my frontal lobe in my brain. He also told me that I had broken three vertebrae in my lower back. I was so fuzzy and out of sorts that none of it really sunk in, but I was so shocked because I couldn't remember a thing. My amazing friend had been coming to visit me every day to check on me since my parents were away at the time. My brother, James, never visited me in the hospital, but he did pick me up, which I suppose is something. Andy never came to see me either which did upset me.

James dropped me back to the yard on my own with an arsenal of pills. The pain was unbearable, and walking was almost impossible. I had a morphine paracetamol mix which absolutely knocked me out. I would sleep all day with only a few brief toilet stops or snack breaks. I would then go back to bed and sleep all night. I lost almost two stone in my recovery over a month. Andy eventually came to see me and stuck by me throughout my recovery and would visit when he could. My family support was lacking somewhat, and I started to wonder if this was because of what I had done and the can of worms I had opened.

I had a month of recovery before the manager of the yard insisted that I come back to work. I was still in so much pain and taking tablets like they were going out of fashion, which was making me so drowsy. It was only when I started working again that I realized how much I was struggling with my memory, organizing, and generally managing the team we had due to my head injury. My back couldn't withstand mucking out or the turning out of horses due to the amount of walking. The manager of the yard had absolutely no sympathy towards me at all and asked why I was so tired after having a month off work. Unbelievably, she even told the owner of the yard that I had only suffered a bump to the head. Never mind breaking my back and causing damage to my frontal lobe. He was totally unaware of my situation, and when I informed him, he was appalled at the manager's behaviour.

It wasn't long before I decided I needed to rethink what I was doing for work. I researched courses that I could do to re-train and decided to take a PA and Secretarial course, which would take me up to London for three months. This was a worry for me because I was getting to grips with the way my brain was working and wondered if learning would be a problem. Unfortunately, taking on this course would mean moving back to my parents' house and commuting daily until I secured a job. The thought of moving back was so daunting. Did I really want to take this all on again and go back to the lies?

Eventually, I was accepted onto the course in London and was set to start that April. This meant handing in my notice at the yard, which went down like a lead balloon. I had a month before I was due to start and moved back into the house, and stayed in the spare room.

As part of my recovery, I was assigned an Occupational Therapist who was going to help me with the transition into my new course. I spoke to her about my memory issues and that I was worried about learning. She told me that she thought the course was a mistake and that I needed to stop trying so hard. I was so upset but also surprised that she would say something like that. It only made me more determined to prove her wrong. I cancelled the sessions as they were too negative.

When I moved home, secrets were everywhere. The atmosphere was unpleasant, and I wasn't sure if I was creating it. I had to find out what He had been up to whilst I had been away. It was now an itch I just has to scratch. I started searching His study and looking at the paperwork. He had taken the profile and password off the computer while I had moved out, so I was able to see some of what He had been doing. He had deleted his history, but there were gambling shortcuts on His home screen again. My heart sank. I couldn't believe He was still doing this, but how bad was it? Was He racking up debt again? Who would bail Him out this time?

Whilst I was coming in and out of the house on the run-up to my course, as soon I approached the study on the way to my room, I would hear a frantic mouse click. He was obviously trying to hide what He was looking at. So, yes, He was still up to no good. Every time I heard it, it made me angrier.

By now, mum was approaching retirement at work and was so excited about the prospect of finishing and having time with friends. Her goal was to eventually sell the house, downsize and be very comfortable for the rest of her life. Things, however, were about to take a very different path.

It was getting so very awkward in the house. The final straw for me was coming home one day. I walked into the house and towards the study. The study was next to the stairs, so I had to walk past it to get to my room. This time though, not only was there the hurried mouse click but also the sound of a belt buckle being done up. I felt sick to my stomach. I ran upstairs and threw up. I sat on the floor in the bathroom in floods of tears, gagging at the thought of what He was up to. My hate for Him grew more and more every single day that I was in that house. How could He do that so blatantly in the family home?

His time was up. I called James because I really didn't want to tackle this alone. I had to tell him what was going on first. I broke it to him gently and only told him what I had found recently. I didn't go back as far as when we were children. He was in complete shock, and to be honest; I'm not sure he believed me. I asked if he could give me some time to come and we could speak to mum together. We would need to try and break this horrible news to her, which would have terrible consequences. He promised me that he would come to the house the following day to sit down with her and do it together. I felt relief at having told him and that he was going to help me.

That night, I went to bed with the weight of the world on my shoulders, my mind spiralling. I must have gone over that conversation about a thousand times. How do you tell your own mother that your father is gay and has been meeting people online and in person? It's like He had a whole other life that He thought no one knew about. It's the kind of stuff you read about, not real life. But now, this was my life, and I was damned if I was going to keep His dirty secrets anymore. On top of that, He was also gambling again.

The next morning, I was still playing out the conversation in my head when my phone buzzed. A message from James. 'I won't be able to make it this evening, I have football.' Are you fucking kidding me? How is football more important than this? Why can't you give me just an hour of your time? Am I seriously going to have to do this on my own? What the hell is wrong with my family, and why can't they confront anything?

By now, you have probably realized that I am not the sort to let things lie. If something needs to be done or said, I will do it. I won't sweep things under the carpet and forget that it even happened.

There was absolutely no way in hell that I was going to delay this conversation. I had made the decision to tell her, and that's exactly what I was going to do. I just had to get the words out somehow.

My mum went to work. I stayed in my room most of the day thinking. I didn't eat because I felt so nauseous, and I was exhausted from lack of sleep. I didn't want to speak to anyone in case I broke down. I honestly think I was as upset about my brother not helping me as I was about Him. It looked like I was on my own.

Before I knew it, I heard my mum's car on the gravel driveway. My heart was in my mouth. I was sweating, and my pulse was going a million miles per hour. It just so happened that He had gone to a 'conference,' and was away for the night. Of course, every time a 'conference' came up, I knew that He had either made plans to be with someone else while He was there or that there actually was no conference and He was playing away.

Well, here goes nothing…

Chapter 3

'A single lie discovered is enough to create doubt in every truth expressed.'

- Unknown

Should I have said anything? I still don't know the answer to this question, but I feel like it has had more of an adverse effect on my life than anyone else's; long-term.

I went into the living room where my mum was sitting, watching her normal soaps on the TV. I asked her if we could have a chat, and instantly, that look of worry again. Her eyes were wide, and her pupils large. I struggled to even look her in the eye. I said, 'I have no idea how to tell you this.' She sat there waiting like I was going to tell her that I had done something unforgivable.

I don't know why, but whenever I tried to get the words out, I would laugh. I think it was out of pure fear, but even now, I think what a strange reaction it was.

I told her that I had been keeping an eye on what He had been up to and that it wasn't good. She asked me if He was gambling again. I told her that it was a strong possibility but that there was more I needed to tell her; I just wasn't sure how.

I told her that there were other things on the computer which I wished I had never found. There were websites, chat rooms, and images of other people. Why was it so hard to get this out? I was so ashamed. I said that the other people were not women and that He had been meeting up with them regularly.

My mum's face dropped. She sat there speechless for what felt like an age. It was only now that the emotions hit me, and my eyes started to well up. I felt sick; I felt guilty and so sad for mum. Why was I feeling guilty, though? Was I going to keep feeling like this? I thought telling her would help, but I felt so much worse.

I kept apologizing because I was spluttering words out just trying to explain. I didn't tell her how long I had known, only that I had discovered these things and she needed to know about it. I felt bad because I was only telling her half the truth, but she needed to know. I didn't want to make it worse for her than it already was.

Eventually, Mum, in tears, thanked me for telling her and said how hard it must have been. She said that she would speak to Him when He came home. That's when it hit me. He is going to know that I told her, that I spilled His vile secrets. What have I done? I felt scared. I still had to live there for the next four months or so while I was on my course. I felt like I had made things so much worse. Strangely though, a little more weight was off my shoulders for having told her, even if it was only a portion of it, but now I felt nerves too.

My mum and I decided to have a look in the study to see if we could find anything. My mum found a load of paperwork about the mortgage on the house. Looking through it, there was a signature on the back from them both. I had a look at it, and I could tell that her signature had been forged. Mum's signature has never changed and is identical every time she signs. I could tell that it was not real.

Reading the mortgage paperwork was just the most horrific thing. Mum was so prepared for the mortgage to be paid in the next few years and to finish work and enjoy life. This was definitely not going to happen any time soon.

It seemed that He had re-mortgaged the house. This was no ordinary mortgage, though. He had signed up for a mortgage which meant that they had been paying interest only for the past ten or so years. On top of that, the fine print stated that, on the sale of the house, the bank would take 60% of the value of the property plus the repayment of the mortgage. I felt like I had just watched Mum's world shatter into a million pieces. As if the news I had just given her wasn't enough. What had He done with the money from the re-mortgage? Had He gambled it? What the hell was going to happen now? Poor mum.

The next evening, He arrived home from his trip. I literally had nowhere I could go to escape. I spoke to Andy and asked if I could come and stay, but he had plans. Having not told him any of what had happened, I suppose he didn't know exactly how much I needed an out. It seems that I didn't trust him enough to confide in him. I ended up going up to my room and waiting for whatever shitstorm was about to come my way.

All I could hear were muffled voices from downstairs. I could tell from her voice that my mum was crying. I didn't hear Him say much, which clearly made Mum so angry. She got louder and louder, waiting for a reasonable response.

Eventually, it went quiet downstairs, and there was a tap on my door. He was asking if He could talk to me. I shouted, 'No, I don't want to talk.' He crept away, and I stayed put. I broke down, knowing that this was going to rip my family apart, and had been the one to do it.

I must have fallen asleep at some point that evening and woke up the following morning to find that He had run off again. I was so angry, and my blood was boiling. I kept hoping that He wouldn't come back. He had done so much damage already that I didn't want Him back, ever!

My mum and I decided to rip the study apart and find out just how bad it really was.

We found a letter about a mortgage indemnity. It looked like this was still in place. We found endless credit card statements for different accounts, which mum knew nothing about. It just went on and on. Piles of paperwork were stacked up, which all needed going through.

Mum was trying to get hold of Him to find out where He was and if He was even still alive. There were no police involved this time. If He was gone, He was gone. We weren't getting another search party out for Him, but she did want answers.

Eventually, Mum received an email from Him. An email! In the email, He said that He had falsified the indemnity letter. There was no insurance on the mortgage. He got the details of the company online and faked the whole letter. He said He owed a lot of money to different lenders but not one word that would suggest an apology.

The email was basically blaming all of us for all His downfalls. It was our fault that He booked and took us on expensive holidays. It was our fault that He bought us expensive presents. Apparently, when we were children, He thought that we expected certain things and that my mum wanted all the holidays. The funny thing is, as children, we didn't expect anything, it was great to get any present we were given. My mum only enjoyed the holidays because she was told that they could afford them. Mum is very savvy with money, so if she thought they couldn't afford it, they would never have gone.

He also wrote in the email that he didn't really want to be around us anymore and was much happier on His own. It was the most infuriating email I have ever read, and the fact that everything He was putting us through was our fault was laughable. What a ridiculous human being.

He didn't come back to the house for almost two weeks after running off. When He came back, He returned to mum, who was demanding a divorce. While He was away, mum had spoken to my Grandparents and told them half the story. She told them only about the mortgage and the debt, nothing to do with His other activities. She would never tell them that their son had been unfaithful. I couldn't believe how much restraint she showed. I was raging every single day and wanted everyone to know how much of an arsehole He was. She was able to put it aside and think of them.

It was decided that because my grandparents were too old to move, we would keep the house on until such time that they had either passed or had to go into a home for full-time care. Although this sounds morbid, mum had to be strong about it. This would mean that mum would have to keep working and put her retirement off. She promised another four years of work because now she was in a position where she would have to look after herself and stop supporting Him. She would have to save her money and organize new pensions to make sure she would have enough to live once she finished work. This did mean, however, that He would still be living in the house. Mum's friends told her to kick him out and ensure He paid his half of the mortgage and bills, which I was in full agreement with. She never did ask Him to leave. This is the first time I lost a bit of respect for her. I wanted her to be selfish and think of herself for once. I think this is when I really started to push her away.

I had to get out of there as quickly as possible. How could I live there after everything I had done? I could feel a huge weight on my shoulders again and so much guilt for unearthing the secrets. I felt like all of Mum's pain was my fault.

Around the same time, James was getting married, which complicated things. For some reason, they invited Him to the ceremony but not the reception. I was so confused at how people still wanted Him in their lives. All I wanted was for Him to leave for good. I invited Andy. He didn't seem overly interested but was going to come anyway.

The day arrived, and it was, as you can imagine, a lot to take in. Andy arrived in a horrendous mood, which made so angry. As if this day wouldn't be hard enough. He was so rude to mum when she was just asking him general questions. I was trying to get him away from talking to anyone because I felt awkward as he was being such an arsehole and I was annoyed that I had even invited him. The awkwardness continued. I had to be in photographs with Him and the rest of the family. I had to pretend like everything was alright and that nothing had happened. I never said a word to Him, though, or even looked in His direction. Fortunately, the ceremony and photos were only a few hours, but it felt like a lifetime.

The reception was more relaxed, but with Andy being in such a bad mood, I decided to have a reasonably early night and go up to the room. It wasn't the day I would have hoped for at all, but at least I hadn't had to speak to Him.

From that point onwards, it seemed like James favoured his wife's family over ours. In a way, I didn't blame him because ours was such a mess, but mum could definitely feel it, and it had started to upset her.

Finally, my course started in London, which meant I was up early and back late in the evening. This made things easier living at home. I would spend the weekends with Andy; he was also now re-training to be a Personal Trainer. He had left the RAF and had a bit more time available. It did feel like things were going in the right direction but going home to a dark cloud in the evenings was so draining.

I worked through my course for three months. I worked so hard to ensure I would get the best grade and be able to get a job in London as quickly as possible to stay away from the house.

I finished the course three months later with a distinction and applied for jobs with agencies. If only I could tell the Occupational Therapist how well I had done, and where to stick her advice. I had an interview for a particular role that a friend of mine had put me forward for. I was offered the role initially, but out of nowhere, it was taken away. I remember sitting in her office while she broke the news. I just cried. It was so embarrassing because she didn't know my situation. I think she just knew that it was my road out of the home. I had to keep looking.

Eventually, I interviewed for a role with a gaming company in Central London. I was accepted for the job and started a week later. It was great and exactly what I needed. A great boss, a great team, and social life. Around the same sort of time, Andy had taken a job at a top gym and been offered a free room at an old barracks in London to be live in security. The barracks was closed as it was being moved to another location in West London. When I took the job, Andy suggested that I move in with him. I jumped at the offer. Closer to the moving date, he seemed to get a little distant, and when it came to me driving all my things up there, he decided to go out, so I had to move in on my own. That should have been a huge red flag, really, and to be honest, I was devastated that he wasn't there to greet me. It felt like it should have been a defining moment in our relationship and worth celebrating, but it felt very short of that.

Living together was alright, but there were things I was starting to notice. He didn't necessarily want me there but going out with my friends from work was causing an issue.

The major reason for me was to be away from home, so I stuck with it, rightly or wrongly.

We decided to look at flats with one of his friends from work to try and keep the rental costs down. We found a place in West London, a maisonette with two bedrooms and a good size kitchen and lounge. We split all the bills, and it worked quite well.

I started training at the gym a lot and trying to get my strength up when I found CrossFit for the first time. I fell in love with it, and it was to become an obsession. I started small in the gym Andy worked at and then eventually joined a CrossFit box with him. Once again, he managed to make me feel awful when he refused to do workouts with me because I was not up to his level of fitness. The point of CrossFit is that you scale the workouts and do what you are able, so we could quite easily have done them together. To broadcast in front of a room of people that he wanted another partner was absolutely humiliating.

We both managed to get an invitation to go and volunteer at a regional CrossFit event in Copenhagen. It was an amazing week of meeting like-minded people and working hard at something we loved.

On the back of the regionals, we were then invited out to help at the CrossFit Games in LA. We jumped at the chance. I worked with the equipment team, and he worked with the athletes. This was probably a good thing because we were apart for a lot of the trip. I made a good friend while I was out there and spent a lot of time with her, which was much more relaxed.

I had taken some dresses and nicer clothes to wear out in the evening or when we went for dinner. Andy had only taken shorts and t-shirts. I put on one of my very casual dresses to go out one evening, and he told me that I was just trying to make him look stupid for dressing nicely and making an effort. I was so hurt that he couldn't just tell me that I looked nice and that we should go out for a nice meal. I was starting to feel as if this relationship was taking a nasty turn.

Our second week in LA was spent traveling around and seeing some of the beautiful beaches and most popular areas. We took a surfing lesson which was great, and I even managed to stand up a few times on my first try. The next morning, we decided to go on our own and try surfing without an instructor. It was much harder due to the size of the waves. When we dropped the equipment back, we were asked how we got on. Once again, Andy decided to try and make me look stupid. He told the instructor that I spent most of my time underwater, laughing about it. When I laughed and said, "so did you," joining in on the joke, he lashed out and said, "Oh, here we go, just because you feel stupid, you need to make me feel stupid too." I was so shocked and embarrassed. The instructor had a look in his eye that I can only describe as pity towards me.

That was it; I was done. I decided to end this as soon as we would get back home. I won't tolerate being spoken like that and made to look like an idiot. He had issues from being in the military that he wouldn't speak to me about. I couldn't help him, and this relationship was turning so sour.

Whilst we were in LA, I had a day with a friend I had made out there. She told me she was looking for a flatmate. I felt like it was meant to be. I told her I would think about it and come back to her as soon as we got home.

We got on our flight home and arrived back in London. We barely said ten words to each other on the way home. I was so cross with the way he had spoken to me; I just didn't want to be near him.

I got home and immediately contacted my friend, saying that I would love to take her spare room. I had to break this to Andy and our flatmate though. I spoke to them both, and instead of a response, Andy got up and walked off to sit in the bedroom, slamming the door behind him. I let him go; there was no way I was going to chase him.

Not even fifteen minutes later, my phone went off, and I had an email from him. An email? I was sitting two rooms away from him. I couldn't believe it! This is exactly what happened to my mum. An email with an explanation for his behaviour because he couldn't have a physical conversation.

There was a list of excuses for the things he had said and the way he treated people. He said that he needed help and needed to confront things, but yet he couldn't confront me. He said that we could live apart but stay together and that he loved me. There was no way I was going to keep a relationship going when I couldn't even live with him. Looking into the future, what kind of relationship would that be? I didn't understand that if he loved me, how could he treat me the way he did? That's not love. He finally accepted the fact that I was leaving and that things were over, and I moved out two weeks later. It was a very atmospheric two weeks, and I felt awful because I was causing it to a degree. Although it was the right thing to break up, I was the one who wanted it. I couldn't wait to get out of there.

I moved in with my friend and joined a CrossFit box just around the corner from our flat. It was bliss. It was fun, relaxed, and healthy in terms of training, eating, and no atmosphere. But soon, the landlord wanted to move back into the apartment, so we needed to find a new flat. We found another maisonette in West London and were ready to move. It was so exciting. We hired a van and were on our way. The flat was lovely. Two double bedrooms and a great open-plan kitchen and living area. It was freshly decorated, and you could smell the paint as soon as you walked in. I liked that smell; it felt new.

It wasn't long before she met someone through CrossFit and started dating. I guess this was when things took a turn. There were times when I would come home, and they were both naked on the sofa in the living room. I was so angry for being embarrassed about walking into my home. They would leave the flat an absolute mess for me to clean up every day. It was so awkward, and I started to feel uncomfortable living there. There was no consideration, and it felt like this was the plan, and that if they tried hard enough, then I would move out, and they could live there together. For me, there was no other explanation.

About six months after moving into the flat, my boss had to break it to me that he was going to have to make me redundant. The company was struggling with competition, and my role was seen as a luxury. This fell on me like a ton of bricks. I couldn't believe it. He gave me as much time as he could to find another job, but because he had been so generous with pay raises, I couldn't find a role that paid the same for my level of experience; Afterall, I had only been in PA work following my qualification for about two years. Most jobs wanted five years plus for the salary I would need. Since I had taken the lease on the flat, I would need the right salary to be able to pay for it. This was a nightmare; what was I going to do?

I managed to find the odd temp job, but eventually, a role came up about thirty minutes from my parents' house back home. They had seen my profile online and wanted to meet with me. The salary was great, and because I had the qualification I gained in London, they were really interested. I decided to take the interview and see what happened. I was offered the job on the spot, and I snapped it up. A brief moment of relief, but now I had a new problem. I had to tell my friend. I would have to tell her that I would need to leave London.

I sat down and spoke candidly with her one evening. She knew that I had been made redundant and that I was struggling to find work. I had eaten through most of my savings paying rent and had no other options. I told her that I had been offered a job back home and that I would have to consider taking it, even though I had basically accepted it. I offered to find a new flatmate for her, someone that she would ultimately choose, but I would pay for the process and administrate the whole thing. Initially, she seemed okay with it and was understanding. I thought I was out of the woods. Of course, by now, you have probably realized that luck is very rarely on my side and that I have a knack for finding the wrong people.

A couple of days passed, and she decided that she didn't want a new flatmate; she wanted me to pay the rent on the flat even though I would not be living there. She said that I had to pay the rent for the remainder of the tenancy. I was mind blown. How can you expect someone to do that, especially when I would have to move and pay rent elsewhere? I would have preferred for her to give up the flat and pay the fee for an early release from the landlord. Sadly, she wouldn't agree to that either. I felt like this was playing into her hands perfectly. She could live with her boyfriend and get monthly payments from me, but without me being in the way. It was the perfect situation for them both.

I chose to seek legal advice. I had offered her so many avenues, which she refused to take. I refused to pay the money while I wasn't there, so she eventually told me that she was taking me to court.

Leaving the flat in this situation, once again, meant moving back to the house for a short time whilst I got something else organized. I agreed with mum that I would pay half the mortgage to enable her to save some money, but first, I would have to sort out the flat in London. I couldn't pay the London prices for a flat plus half the mortgage on a six-bed home. She understood and was grateful for any help.

It wasn't long until I received my letter saying that I was being taken to the small claims court. The date had been set, and she was actually doing this. My luck just keeps getting better and better. I had to prepare. I thought this girl was a friend and would be understanding of my situation. Who would do that? I know that I would never do that to anyone, and I would help in any way I could. Does that make me weak? If I had to find a new flatmate, I wouldn't think twice about it; I would just do it. Was I the only person with a shred of decency left? I was really starting to hate people and lose faith in humanity. Everyone either had an agenda, lied or cheated.

Moving home was awful. I wasn't exactly welcomed, but it was only going to be short-term. I had to start my new job and get my head back into work and training. It was nice to be able to call up some old friends and spend evenings out of the house with them, but now people were of the age where they were settling down, getting married, and having children. This meant a smaller amount of people to call on, but it was still so nice to see them all.

The thought of having children was something that I decided I would never do. I would never want to make a child feel like I did or put so much stress and worry on someone of such a young age. I knew that I wasn't capable of the things that He had done, but I still could never even think about having children. The way I felt about people now, and the way I pushed people away made me feel that I could potentially do that to a child, so I ruled it out completely.

It felt such a relief to be out of London. I was starting to feel claustrophobic and craved trees, fields, and the great outdoors which made me feel so refreshed. I went to visit my friends I used to work with at the yard and managed to get some riding from some of the owners whose horses I used to look after. It was only very gentle hacking, but it was so nice to clear my head. It was the first time I had been on a horse since my accident. I was nervous, but the feeling of freedom and joy was far greater.

I finally started my new job for a big corporate company after numerous security checks. I didn't really want to go into the corporate world but needs must. The team was nice. I connected so well with one of them immediately. She shared my sense of humour, my bad language, and my distain for humanity. She also had so much amazing advice for me. She remains an amazing friend to this day, and I can speak to her about anything. She tells other ways to look at things and pulls me back when I need her to.

I joined a CrossFit box near work and was given a discounted rate by the owner who I used to work with years before. Things felt like they were starting to get somewhere near normality again, apart from the looming court case.

While I was working, I did as much as I could to prepare for my court date. It was fast approaching, and I was getting so nervous about it. I couldn't afford a lawyer but had help from a family friend who tried to give me as much information as possible. I wasn't sure it would be enough, and I worried that I would crumble when it came to it.

The date came around, and a very good friend of mine offered to come with me. It didn't go well. It felt very much like this wasn't the first time she had done this to someone.

She was so prepared to a professional level that I didn't have a hope in hell's chance. The judge was sympathetic to my case and told her that if he could make a moral decision rather than following the law, he would have ruled in my favour. I was now in a position where I would have to pay her a significant amount of money which now included the court fees. To be honest, I was just happy for it to be over. Afterall it's only money, and I can always earn more. I organized a loan to cover the amount I needed, and fortunately, it was in my account in a few days. I was lucky it was so quick because she was chasing me for payment the day after court. I paid what I owed and blocked her from every possible avenue, deleted any friends we had in common on social media, and cut all ties for good. It wasn't long after the court case that I found out she had given up the flat a long time before the case, so she had only paid a fraction of what I had paid her. This was just salt in the wound, and it showed me exactly who she was. I still believe she set out to extort me as she saw I needed help all those months ago in LA. My faith in humanity was basically gone at this point, and the realization of what people were capable of was so upsetting. What a horrible world we live in. Why was it so hard to find genuine people who didn't have an agenda?

Now that the London case was over, the flat was finally sorted and life was on the up again, it was time to start paying half of the mortgage for mum so that she could put some money away into savings. I was happy to do it, but it was a lot more than I would have ever paid for a room or a flat. I felt I needed to do my best though, as I still had a huge amount of guilt hanging over me.

I had been home a few months and decided it was about time that I started to date again. I was feeling a bit lonely as most of my friends were in relationships, and at home, I stayed in my room to avoid Him.

The dating process is so horrible, and you speak to so many strange people before you find any good ones! I even had one person ask for a pair of my running trainers in return for payment! BLOCK!! There are also an incredible number of men with foot fetishes out there. I hate feet… BLOCK!

Living in a small town, the dating scene was much smaller than that of London, so I was going to have to bide my time and wait for the right guy to come along.

I went on one date with a guy. I wasn't sure about him before I even went, but I thought I would give it a go. If anything, I would use it to up my dating game, and it was a night out of the house. It was such an unpleasant experience. He proceeded to analyse everything about me throughout the date and gave me a lovely summary at the end. He couldn't have been more wrong about me. He then asked if I wanted another drink and to tell him what I thought of him. I told him that I wasn't sure that my analysis of him was date-worthy, and I would definitely not like another drink. I also give him some friendly advice. People generally don't like to be analysed unless they are paying someone to do it. And if he was to do it again, he would need to be a lot more accurate. I wasn't rude to him, but really felt that he needed to know. Onwards and upwards, so they say!

I was finding that a lot of profiles online were fake and was debating just giving dating a miss for a while. It was exhausting speaking to all these strange people. With all the people I had to deal with the past few years, I was going to need to find someone very much on my wavelength. I wanted to find someone that I could trust with everything and anything. Someone that adored me and wanted to spend time with me, not finding excuses because they weren't man enough to be honest with me. Honesty was going to be key for me. I was fed up with lies and deceit.

I was just about to cancel my subscription to a particular website when an image popped up. A 6'4 guy with a beard and tattoos called Chris. Now you're talking. He's also a Taurus like me; Maybe that means he's on my wavelength. I sent him a message simply saying, 'please tell me you're real.' I got a message back quite quickly, laughing and telling me a bit about himself and that he most assuredly was real. We both made a plan to get together for a drink that week. I was nervous because this guy was very much my type, and I didn't want to mess this up. I had a gut feeling about him. Before we finished our chat, he said that he had noticed that I was a Taurus and wondered what my date of birth was. I told him and he responded with, 'no way, that's the same as mine.' Honestly, I thought it was a strange chat upline and just played along. Was this a red flag? Was he a total weirdo? I could always check when we met, I thought.

Date night arrived, and I was so nervous. I was going to walk up to the pub to meet him but was worried my hair would be a mess by the time I got there. How girly of me! I was blessed with hair that grows and grows as soon as it senses any kind of moisture. It's not a good look! So, I drove! Chris was stood leaning against his car, looking so handsome and dressed to impress. I parked up, and we met with a kiss on the cheek and a hug. He was so tall. Being 5'11 myself, it was so nice to meet someone that was significantly taller than me. We walked into the pub and got our drinks.

As soon as we got to the table, we sat down next to the open fire, and he flung his driving license across the table with a cheeky grin on his face. His date of birth was exactly the same as mine. What are the chances? I told him that I thought it was a creepy chat upline, and we laughed about it.

We got chatting about where we grew up and where we live now, work and what we did in our spare time, the usual date talk. I told him that one day I would want to move to another country and how much I loved Canada. He was interested in Australia but intrigued by Canada, and agreed that life was too short to spend in one country all your life.

I felt like I wanted to tell him about part of my situation now to get a read on him. I told him that I had moved home after being in London for a few years and that it was awful because I didn't get on with Him. I told him that a 'friend' took me to court, and now I was working close to home and helping my mum to pay her mortgage. A lot to take in for someone you don't know. He sympathized with me but fully understood. He was kind about it, which instantly put me at ease.

Chris used to be close to his mum, but she passed away about nine years before we met. She had been diagnosed with lung cancer and, sadly, didn't have long between diagnosis and her passing. It was a really hard time for him as he was so close to her. His relationship with his dad had never been great but worsened over time as he re-married only a year after his mum's passing. It seemed we had similar relationships with our families, which immediately settled me. He was so easy to talk to, and we talked all evening until the pub was due to close. I didn't want the night to end. He was so good-looking, he had big brown eyes, and his laugh was infectious. I liked him a lot and knew that my gut feeling was right.

It felt like real talk. We laughed and joked about other things, but it felt like a 'this is me, like it or lump it,' kind of a date. For me, it was perfect because we both knew exactly where we stood from day one, and I was honest about my situation, or as much as I have divulged so far. I felt that there were some who would run a mile, but would he?

I went home with a huge smile on my face and sat with mum to tell her all about it. Her smile matched mine, and she could see how happy I was about it. I did tell her that Chris wasn't her choice of a man for me because of his tattoos and beard. I could see her judging instantly, but that's just mum.

He texted me as soon as he got home to tell me that it had been a great night and asked if I would go for dinner with him in two days' time. I had butterflies and was so excited. Of course, I was going for dinner.

On my dating profile, my tagline said that my perfect date would be a day at the zoo because even if the date was rubbish, you could still see all the animals. He found it highly amusing.

So when I met him for dinner he told me that he had booked a trip to Longleat Safari Park for our joint birthday, which was only a few days away. No one had ever done anything like this and never paid so much attention. I felt like my heart was going to burst. What an amazing person. So thoughtful. This night couldn't get any better.

We had our date at the zoo, and it was such fun. I don't think I have ever laughed like that with anyone. Chris got me a birthday card too, and he wrote a message asking me to be his girlfriend. I swear I had tears in my eyes; it was so sweet and exactly what I needed. I needed to be with someone who wanted to be with me. I needed love. It felt like we had known each other for years. We were so similar. I put it down to us both being Taurus and sharing our birthdays.

I started to spend a lot of time at his house. I got to spend time with him and be away from home. It was the little things that made such a big difference. It was warming up my car, ready for me to go to work on cold mornings. It was having dinner ready on the table when I got home or making my lunches to take with me. It was the messages every morning once we had both got to work saying how happy he was and that he loved spending time with me. Where had he been all my life? He was so amazing to me and really, genuinely cared for me. I hadn't felt this amount of love and I felt like I had been cruising through life, missing out.

On Valentine's Day, his gift to me was a beautiful picture of the stars. The image showed the night sky in the exact location of our first date. The image said, 'The night our souls entwined and our lives changed forever.' He just knew what I loved and knew how to make me smile.

Just when things were going so well, I started to have some issues with my neck, which stemmed from my accident all those years before. Since I was kicked in the head, my neck had been damaged, and the vertebrae had deteriorated a little. I was seeing some specialists who suggested

Cortisone injections into my neck to try and reduce inflammation. I had to have one side of my neck injected at a time whilst being under anaesthetic. Chris came with me on both occasions, and waited in my room whilst the injections were done. He refused to leave me on my own and wanted to be there to make sure I was alright.

Sadly, the injections had no effect at all, and by now, the headaches that were stemming from my neck pain were unbearable. Some days they would have me in tears because no amount of painkillers or anti-inflammatories would kill the pain. The next step with my specialist was to have a nerve block. This would be a very long needle going through the front of my neck to reach the nerves at the back. This was all done whilst I was awake, and quite honestly was the most horrendous experience. I felt the needle touch the nerves and could feel spasms in my face and all the way down my arm to my hand. It was excruciatingly painful. Chris came with me to that appointment too, and waited while I recovered. He was so worried because the procedure had scared me, and I got quite upset about it.

Eventually, I got so frustrated with my specialist for not helping me that I took to Facebook to ask my friends for recommendations of someone who may be able to help with alternative therapy and pain management. I was given the name of an Osteopath in Windsor. He practised medical acupuncture, massage, and chiropractic therapy, amongst other things. He had looked after the British Olympic rowing team previously, so I booked in to see him. After my very first session, I was pain-free. My head cleared, my jaw loosened, and the tension in the back of my head was gone. One session! I couldn't believe it. It had taken me months to have the numerous injections, but one session using nothing but hands and acupuncture needles, and I was feeling amazing. When I asked my specialist if I could be referred to the Osteopath so that I wouldn't be paying a fortune each time, they refused the request because he didn't believe in alternative therapies. It was safe to say that I was going to have to pay for the sessions myself, which were expensive but so worth it to be pain-free.

Some time passed, and I spent more and more time at Chris' house. I was still paying my mum's share of the mortgage, but she could see that I was so happy with Chris. She said that if I wanted to move into his house, she would release me from her payments, and I could get on with my life with him. I had covered about a year of her payments so she had saved a good amount of money. It was a godsend. I spoke to Chris and told him the news, and the next time I went over, he handed me a front door key. It bought tears to my eyes. This meant more to me than he would ever know. Were things starting to come together for me?

It dawned on me that our relationship was so honest, yet he didn't know all my secrets. It started to weigh me down again. I thought I was going to need to tell him everything, even the deepest darkest things. Afterall, I was having days when I was feeling frustrated because things were getting on top of me, and I felt I owed it to him to explain my behaviour.

We had a quiet night in, and I told him that I needed to talk to him and that these things were hard to talk about. That same look came across his face as my mum when I told her everything. I desperately wanted to stop seeing that look. I explained all the things that I had found, the things that I had to break to my family, and how guilty I felt about all of it. I got so upset whilst I was talking about it and felt embarrassed. He comforted me and listened with no judgment. He fully understood why I hadn't told him before. He told me that I shouldn't feel guilty and that none of it was my fault. He said that I needed to stop taking responsibility for it and that other members of my family should see it from my perspective.

At that moment, when he was holding me while I cried, I loved him so much. I was so happy to have been honest with someone about it all, and I felt that he could be trusted to keep my secret. I could trust him with literally anything.

Soon after, I was offered a new job at work in a new department which I decided to accept. I would be a PA for two department heads in the franchise area of the business. I was getting ready to sign all my paperwork, but it was taking so long to come through. I wondered if it had been sent to my old address, my parents' house. On my lunch break, I drove back to the house to see if it had arrived. I knew mum was away with friends, so I would just pop in and out quickly to check the post and head back to work.

When I got to the house, there was another car on the drive. It was so strange because no one ever visited unless my mum was there. I parked up and went in the back door, which was still locked. This was also strange because any visitors would come to the back, and we all used that door to come and go, so why was it still locked at lunchtime when someone was here? I walked into the kitchen, and there was a man I had never seen before standing there. He was just stood there cooking breakfast. He couldn't have been more than twenty years old. Who the hell was this? Suddenly, from around the corner, He came rushing in. He looked like a dear in the headlights. I looked at him; I was shaking with anger because it was clear that He had a secret visitor while mum was away, and now they were about to have a nice breakfast together. It was clear this man had spent the night in the family home! How disgusting! How could He do that to mum? He literally had no respect for her whatsoever. I quickly walked round to the post box and found my mail, then walkout out of the house as fast as I could. I couldn't even look at Him; I just kept my head down. I felt sick and could hardly breathe. My heart was beating ten to the dozen. I got out of that driveway as quickly as I could.

I called Chris and told him, in absolute hysterics, what had happened. He couldn't believe it. He was so shocked. I told him I was going to have to tell my mum again! She was in France, but I called anyway. I explained to her what was going on and she was appalled. Once again, I had caught Him; once again, I was the one to tell His secret. I was so tired of all of this. I was physically and mentally drained. Mum said that she would talk to Him when she got home the following day.

I went back to the office, excused myself, and said I had received some awful news. I tried to keep it together on the way out so as not to cause a scene. I left and headed back to Chris's house to try and calm down and clear my head. I sat and cried for about an hour. Why was it always me that caught him? Why did I have to tell mum every time? She must hate me by now. Eventually Chris got home and calmed me down.

I had another sleepless night worrying about mum. I was worried about the conversation she was about to have with Him. This was just going to escalate things again after it had been so quiet.

That evening, I received an unexpected text from Him. He was actually threatening me! He said that if I didn't stay out of his business, He would make my life a living hell. He told me to keep my mouth shut and to stay away from Him.

I was so angry, so upset, and hurt! How could He blame me for all of His mistakes, all of His stupidity? I hated Him so much. He had messed up so much of my young life, my trust in people, and my faith in humanity. It had shaped me into the person I was becoming. I felt like all the hairs on the back of my neck were standing up, but I felt hot because my blood was boiling. I felt like I wanted to throw something or hit something. So much rage was running through my body. He was a complete sociopath.

I forwarded the message to my mum and told her I was done. I would never be near Him or speak to Him again. He was no father to me, and the way He treated her was completely unacceptable. Especially after she allowed Him to stay living in the house after everything He had done. I made the decision to completely write Him out of my life for good. The way He was able to treat his own daughter was appalling. At the time, she understood and felt so sad for me.

My brother James had managed to escape any form of confrontation with Him and had kept his head down. He didn't want to take sides and was not willing to discuss things with me. He didn't sympathize with me at all. It almost felt as if he thought I was making it all up and I had caused all the problems myself.

I talked to Chris about it a bit, but I was distraught. Not only had I split up my family, but I also now couldn't go back to the house, James didn't have much to do with me anymore, and it felt like all the blame was on me. The worst thing is, though, I actually blamed myself. I wish I had never said anything.

James and his wife spent more time with her side of the family as if me and mum didn't really exist anymore. They had both become very materialistic, and their lives revolved around who had the best house or car and who earnt the most money. It all just felt very cliquey to me. It was a shame because I never really saw James as that kind of person. I think because me and Chris didn't fit into that mould, we couldn't spend time together.

I spiralled down quite quickly. I was mortified about the way He could send me such a message; I was worried about the effect all of this was having on my relationship with Chris, and I was so frustrated that rather than kicking Him out of the house, mum decided to keep Him there. Why was no one making Him accountable? Why was He not taking responsibility? Because there were no consequences for Him, it made me question everything I had done. Was I right to have said anything each time? Should I have kept quiet and let the lies continue? Why do I feel so awful about all of this when I have done nothing wrong? All I have ever done is to be honest.

Chapter 4

'She was powerful not because she wasn't scared but because she went on so strongly despite the fear.'

- Atticus

Chris and I sat down and really talked. That was what we were so good at. We were such a great team. He said that he was concerned about me and that I was so up and down emotionally. He gave me some tough love, which is exactly what I needed. We talked about Cognitive Behavioural Therapy. I had been thinking about it for a while, but it would mean reliving everything again. I was prepared to give it a go, get someone's opinion on how I was feeling, and maybe find a way to deal with it more effectively and more positively.

I spoke to an old friend who I knew had been to some CBT sessions, and she gave me the number of a lady close to where I was working. I called to book an appointment immediately and started with four sessions. I was so scared about speaking to her, but I knew it was all confidential, and she could never tell anyone. I also didn't want to show emotion or weakness to a stranger. Silly really.

I turned up to my first session. This was it. The whole thing from the start, all over again. I began by telling her from the very beginning, the day we found the magazine when we were so young. She never said a word as I sat there and reeled everything off. I told her how guilty I was feeling about everything. I told her that I hated the fact that the rest of the family was still giving Him their time, but not me. Why did James want a relationship with Him? She hit the nail on the head. She said that he hadn't seen what I had seen. He hadn't had to break the news to people. He kept his distance from most of the situations so that he could be distant mentally too. She was right. He could never understand how I was feeling, no matter how hard I tried to explain it to him. Honestly, I don't think he wanted to understand. Family trait – sweep it under the carpet and live in denial. I am not wired that way, and I never will be. I deal with situations, and I will always speak the truth, no matter how hard it may be.

I was quite shocked that I didn't get overly upset when I talked to her. I felt relief. I think mainly because she didn't react to it as I had expected. She sat and told me that the way I felt was absolutely justified. I am allowed to feel angry. I am allowed to feel hurt, and I am also allowed to feel guilty, even though I shouldn't. She told me that none of it was my fault and that we would work on finding ways to think about it differently.

We set up exercises for when I was feeling low and overthinking things. She gave me things that I could do to help me sleep, such as meditation apps to listen to before bed which would help. Tiredness wasn't helping my emotions at all and was making me run down. It was all very positive, and I recommend CBT and her to so many people.

On my last session, it was on the run-up to Christmas, and I was feeling particularly emotional. I found out that James had invited my mum and Him around to spend the day with them as a family. We would not be invited because of my relationship with Him. I couldn't believe that He was being given a place with the family over Christmas, and we weren't. I couldn't make sense of it at all.

I sat with her and explained it all. I was so upset, even more than I thought. I was in floods of tears, and I couldn't understand why I was so different in this session. She told me that Christmas is the worst time to be dealing with things like this because it's always seen as family time. She confirmed that it was normal to feel this way and to try the exercises we had worked on. She told me to enjoy my Christmas with my lovely boyfriend and take the time to relax. Unfortunately, this was to change Christmas for me in the future. It never felt the same and would sadly drag up old memories every year.

I spoke to Chris about the session and that I felt good to get it out of my system and get the emotions out. I felt lighter and felt that the sessions had made a difference in my outlook on things. She told me that I had to make a decision about how to move on. Did I want to see Him again to try to get an apology and work things out to ultimately have a relationship, or did I want to cut Him out of my life for good? I knew that I would never get an apology. He was not capable of offering me that. I don't believe He thinks He has done anything wrong. I knew that I would need to cut Him from my life and try to move on. I was glad to have made my decision, and I was going to stick to it. It all felt very final. I now had to get over the fact that the rest of my family still wanted Him around and would choose him over me.

Christmas passed, a new year had begun, and things had settled down again. I was glad to start fresh with a clear head. Months passed with no bad news. Our birthdays were coming around, but Chris was acting strangely. I started to worry that something was going on. He seemed secretive and a bit distant. I really didn't want this relationship to come to an end. I was so in love with him. I just wanted him to be as close to me as he was before. What had happened?

Around the same time, my grandpa had become very ill and was being moved to a hospice. He had been diagnosed with bone cancer which had spread to his spine. He was in such agony and was not long for this world. It was such an awful end to an incredible life.

Because he was still at the house, I was unable to visit him there. I was also unsure about what the family had told him about me, so I felt nervous about being near them. I thought I would have been painted me in a bad light and that everything was my fault.

Once he was moved to Phyliss Tuckwell, I was told by my family that it was probably best not to visit him. He was on so much medication to ease his pain and suffering that he wasn't aware of people and his surroundings. This meant that I never got to see him before he passed and never got to say goodbye. This was so awful because he was such an amazing person, and I should have been able to see him. I wanted to be like him one day, and had the same desire to help people and care for people as he did. I decided that because I couldn't see him, I would speak at his funeral. Of course, at the funeral, I would have to see those that I didn't want to see again. I wrote some things down that I felt were a good representation of his character and would ring true to other family members.

I attended the funeral, and it was such a shame that the atmosphere was so horrible. So many people there who knew the financial side of what He had done, yet everyone was pretending it was all fine. It was nice to see my other family members.

I got up and said my piece. It was so hard to do without crying, but I have definitely had to talk about worse things in my life. My mum, Aunty, Uncle, and cousins were complimentary and said it was a lovely tribute to him. I had managed to avoid any contact with Him throughout the whole day, but I was aware that it must have looked odd to other family members. They must have been wondering what was going on.

My granny was also not well. She was struggling with her mobility, and with my grandpa gone, she was not doing well. She came to the funeral but found it very hard because grandpa was all she had day to day. It would be so lonely for her without him. My granny soon got to the point where she was getting muddled and unable to move. Her hips were degenerating, and on one side, the ball of the 'ball and socket joint' was basically gone. She had a walking frame, but her stubbornness meant that she would attempt to move around without using it.

There was one evening when she had two falls in one night. The first time, she was helped up and made comfortable by paramedics. She refused to go to a hospital because she knew that she would never leave to come home. The second visit bought a very tough paramedic who wouldn't take no for an answer and got her to the hospital. I think their level of stubbornness was well-matched, and granny didn't stand a chance. Once at the hospital, she had to perform certain tasks to see if she would be able to look after herself. They eventually concluded that she would need full-time care, so a nursing home would be the only option. A nice home was found for her to move to, which was close to home, so visits would be easy.

This, of course, freed up mum to start the process of selling the house. She knew that she would need to pay back a significant amount of money to the bank, but she had drawn up an agreement whereby she would take the majority of what was left due to being put in this situation unknowingly. Things were starting to look up for her, and she was excited at the prospect of moving.

Me and Chris had been meeting my mum in cafés so that I wouldn't need to go to the house. It made things much more manageable. We went to a lovely garden centre to have a coffee and a cake and a good catchup. Chris still seemed on edge, which I found strange. He was jittery and highly strung. For a very relaxed person, this seemed so out of place. Mum was asking what we wanted for our birthdays and asked about any future plans we had. We told her that we had booked an amazing holiday to Cuba in October. We were so excited. Two blissful weeks, just the two of us. She was excited for us and glad that we had planned something together. It was so nice to see her, and we were so glad that she was doing well. I was excited about her plans to move but just worried that she wouldn't have enough money to get by, but the house was on the market, and they were waiting for a buyer. Although it was a lovely house, it would need work, time, and patience. It needed a very specific person.

On the morning of our birthdays, Chris presented me with a huge box. It was so exciting because he was so thoughtful. I opened it to find another box, and inside that, another. It was endless until I got to a very pretty, small box nestled right in the middle. My heart was racing, and as I opened it, the words, 'will you marry me?' left his lips. My jaw literally dropped. I was so shocked that he was asking me. I said, 'of course, I will,' and gave him a huge hug. I was so excited. He was so emotional. I had never seen that kind of emotion from him which made me feel that it meant a lot.

He had gone to so much trouble, which would be the explanation for his strange behaviour. He had given me his mum's wedding ring and had it re-modelled to my taste in palladium. It was so beautiful, and the fact that he had entrusted me with something so dear to him meant so much more. He had taken months working with a jeweller trying to get it perfect for me. He succeeded. Could this guy get any better? I hit the jackpot with him. He knew everything about me, and it was ok. There was nothing he didn't know, no judgment, just love, and trust. How many people can say that about their relationships?

I was most shocked because when we first started dating, he said that he had been put off marriage and never saw himself getting married. He saw that his dad had re-married so quickly after his mum's passing. It made him question love and if it was all real. He told me that I had made him realise that love is real and that he wanted to spend the rest of his life with me. I was so touched that he felt like that about me and so happy because I felt the same way. I had never felt like this before.

Chris had to go to work that day, but I had the day off as a perk from work. I went to the supermarket and bought some champagne and a couple of lovely steaks for the evening. He got home, and we started cooking up a feast. Suddenly, there was a knock on the door. We looked at each other, wondering who it was. Chris's dad was standing there with a bottle of red wine and a card. He wandered in without wishing me a happy birthday and was unaware that we had planned to have a quiet evening to celebrate. I was so annoyed that he invited himself around without asking and that he didn't even say a word to me when he walked in. He drank his wine whilst we ate, which felt awkward. We told him about the engagement, and his reaction wasn't overwhelming. We showed him the ring, and again, it wasn't the reaction we expected. He stayed until past 11 pm when we both had work the following day, and it put a bit of a downer on our special day. But I still had such exciting news to tell people at work.

We started to plan what we would do for our big day. Neither of us wanted a big affair with lots of fuss. We wanted a few people, if any, to join us to celebrate. Our families were both a bit of a disaster, so we were at a loss for what to do. As soon as we had announced it, people were saying things like, 'I'd better be invited,' and 'I'm a vegan.' The list went on, and it was frustrating us straight away because it all took the day away from us and made it about everyone else. I was not keen on that at all, and neither was Chris.

We went to have some drinks and a BBQ with a friend, and she told us that she got married whilst she was away on holiday in St. Lucia. This instantly sparked something in both of us. We already had a holiday booked, so we both discussed whether we could have our wedding while we were away, on a beach like we both wanted. It felt perfect.

I set about contacting the hotel and trying to find out if they would offer beach weddings. They came back to me quite quickly, sending their packages for our day. We wanted a beach wedding, very simple, close to the jetty by the hotel. It was so easy to organize, and we got it all booked. The next task would be to break the news to my mum. I knew that this would be difficult and that she would be upset that we were eloping. This would really make the light shine on James again, who had a huge wedding with the whole family invited.

My mum was in the process of moving into her new house. She had managed to sell the family home and pay off what she needed to, and had found a lovely little three-bed terraced house. Sadly, her stepmother had passed away, but she had left mum quite a significant amount of money which came at just the right time to allow her to be mortgage free.

Sometimes, I think things happen for a reason and at the right time, as morbid as it sounds. It feels as if life has a plan.

We went to visit her at her new house for lunch one weekend and were prepared to break the news. I just had to be brutal because, at the end of the day, it was what we wanted. I was fed up trying to do things for other people, only for it to backfire on me. Chris could see I was getting nervous about it, so he jumped in and said that he was thinking about whisking me away to be married in Cuba. Straight away, I could see tears in her eyes. She was devastated. She wanted to see her daughter walk down the aisle, but I explained how I felt about everything. I said, "I don't want Him there; I don't want James to give me away, I just want our day to be about us and no one else." She did understand. She even offered to pay for half of my wedding dress which was such a nice gesture considering all things.

We didn't have a huge amount of time, so I organized a day to go shopping with mum to look at dresses. We booked an appointment at a small local shop in town which would only have one person in at a time. I obviously had a budget and a type of dress in mind based on where we would be. I wanted a slim-fitting dress with a low, open back. I had a look at the sale rail and picked a few to try on. The fifth one I tried was a stunning Stella York dress and was so beautiful needing minimal alterations. It had a gorgeous long train and a transparent lace back. I thought it was the one but went to try on some others, too, just to be sure.

We visited a big outlet where dresses were cheaper. They have lots of the same dresses in different sizes, so they didn't have the feel of individuality at all. I gave it time and tried on a few in my size. They felt so generic and standard; they just didn't stand out to me or make me feel as special as I wanted to.

I called the first shop and asked them to put the dress aside and I would come back to get it. I was done in one day, very decisive, and I loved it so much. I thought it was something that Chris wouldn't expect, too, which helped my decision. All I needed to do was to arrange my alterations. Easy!

Chris and I had decided that maybe it was time to start looking at buying our own home together rather than renting. We began to look at areas and developments that we could afford. We looked at schemes that would help us to get on the property ladder. We found one three-bed house that we were keen on and spoke to the sales office. They said that for not much more money, we could get the next house up because it had £60,000 knocked off, 10% cash back, and all of our stamp duty paid for us. We went and had a look at the show home elsewhere because the one we were interested in wasn't built yet. We loved the house. We went back to the sales office and asked if we could put our names down for it.

We felt crazy getting married and looking at buying a house all at the same time, but it felt so right. It was time to get to work.

I called my mum to tell her the news, and she was so excited for us. I think she felt that things were coming together for me too. We got a broker and a solicitor on board and started the process. My mum would lend us some of our deposit money to make sure we could get there on time. Afterall, the 10% cashback would mean we could pay her back straight away. The process meant that we would move into the house in February / March time. It meant we had time. It meant we could go on our amazing holiday without having to worry too much. It meant we could concentrate on our wedding and have a relaxed two weeks together.

Off we went on our flight to Cuba. We stayed in the Cayo's, which are the islands just off the mainland. It only had hotels on it; no one lived there. It was so beautiful. Crystal clear waters, flamingos outside our hotel, and a very short walk to the beach. The heat was intense but so welcome after leaving the cold in the UK. The people were so friendly and couldn't do enough for you.

We had been meeting with the organizer for our wedding at the hotel, and everything was in place for the start of the second week. The manager from the hotel was great. He would go around and speak to all the guests at dinner and make sure they were happy. He came to speak to us, which is when we told him that we were getting married at the hotel and how much we were looking forward to it. He was so happy for us and said that he was going to give us a gift. We didn't really think anything of it until the following day when we got a phone call to our room. The lobby staff asked if we could pack all our things and meet them at the lobby. We were so confused and worried that we had done something wrong. They collected our luggage and loaded them onto golf carts, and drove us out towards the beach. We pulled up outside some gorgeous little buildings just steps from the white sands. They announced that one of these rooms would be our home for the remainder of our stay. We couldn't believe it. It was so quiet and peaceful. All you could hear were the waves lapping. It was such a lovely gesture and such an amazing addition to our holiday. Things couldn't have gotten any better.

We went on some amazing trips while we were there. We went on a jeep safari which took us to some stunning places. We learned how poor Cuba was; it was truly eye-opening. We were told that the way to spot whether a family had a little more money was to look and see if their horse wasn't too skinny. If the horse had more weight on it, it meant that they had two horses and would swap them each day to use for work. Cars were only owned by the rich, the government, or taxi drivers. It really was another world.

We also went on a snorkelling trip on a boat. It was so beautiful. We saw so many fish, and the water was so clear and warm. We even got to swim with a nurse shark.

We would get up early some mornings to watch the sunrise and go down to the beach in the evening to watch it set. It truly felt like paradise.

The day came around for our wedding. I was so nervous but so excited. It was the hottest day so far, and there wasn't a cloud in the sky. It was so perfect.

I checked my phone in the room before getting ready and had so many messages from friends wishing us luck. I had one text that I was definitely not expecting. It was from Him. He wished me luck and said that He was pleased that I was having the beach wedding I always wanted.

I was so angry that He had texted me since the last one I got from Him had nothing but threats and abuse. What was going through His head? It really put me on the back foot and messed with my head a bit. I really didn't want to think about Him that day, but there He was, right in the back of my mind again. I sat down and took a deep breath, and remembered all the things I worked on in my CBT sessions. It was all coming back to me, and I managed to put a positive spin on the situation. He wasn't there. He couldn't ruin my day. None of my family were there to remind me of anything. This was our day and it was going to be perfect.

We had become friends with an older couple at the hotel. I asked her to help me with my dress, which made her day because she only had ever sons, so never had the opportunity to help a bride. It also meant that Chris had a friend on the beach with him while he waited for me. Typically, the air conditioning in our room has stopped working, so getting my dress on was a struggle. Lots of breathing in and cold water, but eventually, I was in.

I walked barefoot down the beautiful gangway towards the white sandy beach on my own, but I wouldn't have it any other way. There is no one that I would want to walk with me or to give me away. Originally, I always thought it would be my brother, but I guess things change over time. Although I was alone, I have never felt stronger. I was doing this on my own, I was doing this for me, and I felt amazing in my beautiful dress. It's funny the things that empower you.

We had a version of Halleluiah playing by Alexandra Berke as I started the long walk down towards my future husband on the beach. We had not expected to have so many spectators, but the whole of the hotel had shown up, and neighbouring hotels had taken up camp on the beach. So many people wished me well on my walk, some clapped for me, and some ladies had tears in their eyes. It was so lovely. There were some Italian ladies taking photos of me, so excited about my dress. I felt like a celebrity. It felt special and was so much fun.

I finally reached the beach and met Chris, who had been standing there so patiently. He looked emotional, and he told me I looked absolutely beautiful. Of course, a nice tan helped things, I think.

The ceremony was short but so personal and private, except for all the onlookers, but they knew nothing about us, which was so nice. We had a very strange Cuban wedding cake which we took back to the poolside bar with us, and we had our photos on the stunning jetty with the clear blue waters in the background. We had such fun and laughed throughout. We weren't nervous anymore, just so happy.

The temperature had got up to about 38 degrees, so once the photos were done, we went back to the room and put swimming costumes on ready to jump in the pool. I had ordered a personalized bikini that said, 'Mrs. K,' on the back of the bikini bottoms. Chris loved it and laughed so hard. We were both so happy, didn't have a care in the world, and were so ready to start our married life together, starting with another six days in Cuba. Bliss! We went and jumped in the pool and got a cocktail from the bar to celebrate.

We had the most relaxing time for the next couple of days. I thought I should check in on emails and progress with our broker and solicitor regarding the house. There it was… an email from the housing developer saying that our moving date had been moved forward, so we would now need to be ready financially to move in just before Christmas.

We both questioned whether this was legal, and we asked the developer if we couldn't wait until our original predicted dates of February / March time. They basically said that if we didn't want the house, they could sell it again. We were mind blown. After being so nice when putting our names down for the house, they were now being so pushy and rude. We were going to have to make this work if we wanted that house.

After wanting a relaxing last few days in Cuba, we were now looking at stress, organizing things from afar with terrible Wi-Fi. What a nightmare, but a nightmare in paradise at least.

I managed to get our solicitor moving more quickly, and we had a few things to sign and agree on. When we got back from the holiday to freezing temperatures, most things were in place; we just needed to sort out our deposit with Mum. She moved the money over to our account straight away. I was so aware that this was a lot of money for her. She was so happy to be able to help us in some way and wished she could give it to us rather than lend it. Everything was ready to go.

Chapter 5

'Life is full of ups and downs. The trick is to enjoy the ups and have courage during the downs'

– Unknown

The completion date on the house would be the 18th of December, but we wouldn't be able to move until we took time off work during the Christmas break. We hired a van for the 27th of December so that we could move after Boxing Day. Our Boxing Day was spent sitting on the kitchen floor packing boxes and wrapping plates and glasses. It's amazing how long it takes to pack your life up. It was exciting, though, if not a little stressful.

It took about three trips in the car and the van, and all day to move everything over. Getting the bigger pieces of furniture in the house was challenging, but we got there. As long as we had a sofa, a bed, and the TV was plugged in, all we wanted to do was get a takeaway and relax for the evening. In a way, it was a good distraction from the other things going on over Christmas, such as the family getting together without us. I have to say; I don't think I gave it much thought. Christmas had been tainted now anyway, so it would never be the same exciting time of the year again.

After being in the house for a while, we started to notice why the house had been finished so quickly. The walls were totally unlevel, so much so that the furniture wouldn't sit in a corner properly. The tiling on the floor in both bathrooms was cracking and lifting; there were sharp hard lumps under all the carpets; they had fitted the windows and French doors without taking the stickers off the UPVC and used silicone to glue it all in place. The list was endless. We would have our work cut out for us for the next six months, trying to get it all fixed.

We told the developer all of our issues, and they started to resolve some of them. They had to take the flooring up in both bathrooms so that it could be re-laid and re-grouted. This meant that the toilet in the family bathroom would have to be removed so that they could put the new flooring down. They re-laid the floor and had the plumber come out to re-fit the bathroom suite. We thought everything was fine until the shower in our ensuite bathroom was tripping the electrics. Chris went down to go and check the issue. He went into the utility room and checked the boiler. We hadn't noticed as we weren't in there much, but there was water dripping down the walls behind the boiler and cupboards, staining the walls. This must have been happening for about three weeks since the bathroom above it had been re-fitted. We were fuming. We spoke to the developers again, who played it down and said they would fix it. They came to see it and told us it wasn't that bad and that it needed to dry before they fixed it. They wanted to wait another three weeks. We couldn't believe it. We were so angry.

The day before the developers were due to come out, Chris decided to take the cupboards down in the utility room so that things weren't damaged by their team, who seemed to be a little incompetent. The minute Chris took them down, the black mould appeared, which had probably been hiding behind the cupboards for three weeks. There were also huge hammer holes in the walls where the electrician had been looking for cables in the walls. Absolutely unbelievable. I was so angry. We had been breathing in this mould for weeks now. Once again, the developers played it down. 'It's not that bad' was the go-to line for them.

The contractors had to take off all the damaged plasterboard and start again in there. It was a nightmare and so frustrating in a brand-new house, which you expect to be perfect.

We decided to hire a company to put some fitted wardrobes in our bedroom. They did a great job. They also built us two nightstands, one of which would sit in the corner of the room, on my side of the bed. When we went to place them, my nightstand wouldn't sit right. It looked like the whole wall was at a horrendous angle when it should have been at 90 degrees. When I spoke to the housing developer, the lady asked if we were sure that the furniture was actually square. Of course the furniture was square. Typically, they try to blame everything on somebody else.

Once again, when the contractors came out, they said that they would fix it and that they would get a master plasterer in to level the wall. We would have to sleep on the floor in the spare room whilst this work was done because we didn't want to have to take our bed apart again for fear it would never be re-built again as it was getting old.

Well, I have never seen such shoddy work in my life. He plastered not only the wall, but the carpet. He splattered it everywhere, all over our new wardrobes, and then washed his bucket out in our bathtub and left the whole thing with a horrible brown mess. There were gaps around the edges of the new wall where he hadn't added enough plaster. It looked horrendous. By this point, I felt like I was about to completely lose the plot with someone. I was so tired and fed up of the constant battles to get our house right.

I called their customer service department and reeled off all the issues we had with the house. They had the cheek to offer us £150 of John Lewis vouchers. So, me being me, I took to social media and tagged them on Facebook, Twitter, Instagram, and any other platform I could get my hands on until I got a reaction from them. I wanted people to know what they were buying when taking on one of these houses, and the lack of workmanship involved. The houses were thrown up so quickly to make as much money as possible. You would think spending half a million pounds would be enough to buy you a well-built property.

Eventually, I received an email saying that the developers were very sorry for these issues, and they offered us £1500 compensation. I didn't think we would be able to get more from them, and honestly, I was tired of it consuming so much of my life. We took the money and decided that any further issues would be dealt with by us so that we wouldn't have anyone in the house who would potentially make things worse.

We decided that we were going to make the house our own and different from all the other houses on the estate. This would not be our forever home, so we wanted to make as much money on it as possible when it came time to sell. We would start with our kitchen-diner. We wanted to have an exposed brick wall at one end as a feature, but it seemed to be costly due to the bricks. Chris took to eBay and found a listing of beautiful handmade bricks. They were over in Oxford, but there was enough for us to do the whole wall. The listing was only £1, so he put a bid on them and we waited patiently.

A few days later, the listing came to an end, and we won the bricks. The seller contacted Chris and said, '£1 per brick, yes?' Chris replied with a firm no, and said that the listing had said £1 for all bricks. The seller told us to pay the pound, bring him some jam doughnuts, and we would be square. We couldn't believe our luck. We just had to go and collect them which would take two trips, but it was worth it.

We built our beautiful wall. Of course, my mum doubted that it would work, and didn't think it would look right. We put an LED strip light hidden above the brickwork so that the light would drop down the wall, and show all the imperfections on the old hand made bricks. It looked incredible. We were so happy with ourselves. Even mum approved and was actually impressed. It can be hard to impress her at times.

We had decided that because our kitchen was looking so lovely, we would offer to host Christmas for Mum, my brother, and my sister-in-law. It did feel like James thought he had to come and that it was a big ask.

Mum decided to take us all to a Christmas light show before Christmas that year at Kew Gardens. We went for a nice dinner first and then for a long walk around the exhibit. It was lovely. It was cold and felt really Christmassy.

We took some nice photos and had a nice evening. I uploaded my pictures with mum and Chris onto my social media, along with photos of James and my sister-in-law, and described it as a lovely evening.

Later that day, James uploaded his pictures of the night, but Chris and I did not feature in any of them. It was like we weren't even there. I was so surprised and didn't really understand the logic behind it. Did he really not want me around that much that he would cut me out of family gatherings on his socials? I was really hurt.

I would have loved to have a relationship with my brother. After all, everything we had to deal with should have brought us closer. Instead, I think that he blames me for the issues in the family. He blames me for having a fractured relationship with Him, and he blames me for everything that has happened in the past years. I was going to try and rekindle something and try to make an effort to fight for a relationship of some sort.

We spent a lot of money on food and alcohol to host a lovely day. We got a big turkey and some tomahawk steaks to have as an extra. The food was amazing, and Chris did so well to prepare it while I doused everyone with alcohol.

The night was going well, and everyone seemed happy. Normally at Christmas, we would keep chatting and drinking late into the evening, but at about 8:00 pm, James said that they had to get back home. I later heard that it was an excuse to get out to go to his wife's parents' house for drinks. I wish they could be honest about things and not sneak around. I hate dishonesty, and I hate feeling like we are second best. They felt that they had a better offer elsewhere, so off they went. It felt as if they had used us for a good meal and then taken the party elsewhere.

Mum stayed a little longer and left at around 11 pm. She had a nice evening with us all and would spend Boxing Day at James'. We were not invited. It did feel like trying to create my relationship with my brother was going to be a challenge and completely one-sided. Chris told me that I should stop trying. It was causing me more pain trying and failing than if I did nothing at all. He was right. I was getting so upset by it all that it wasn't worth my time. So that's what I did. After all, when your past is so present, how can there be a future.

Chapter 6

'If you don't build your dream, someone else will hire you to help them build theirs.'

– Dhirubhai Ambani

Chris and I spent more time doing work on our house. Chris built me a great Hollywood mirror for our bedroom which I loved, and we decided to build a TV wall in our lounge to make it a real feature and to hide all of our cables and TV boxes.

Chris built an amazing frame on the wall, and we found some beautiful teak tiles to clad the frame with. We went to a reclaim yard and found a stunning piece of Yew to have as a shelf for our sound bar. It was an absolute triumph. It looked great.

I discussed with Chris that we should build some reclaimed furniture and clocks and he loved the idea. I set up an Instagram page with the things we had done so far, with progress pictures and future ideas. We started getting a lot of followers. We thought about buying some old cable reels and making huge clocks out of them. They would be simple but so effective. Chris made the first one, and I bought him a solder so that he could burn the numbers into the wood.

We sold the first one so quickly. I wanted to be a part of this, so I made the next one. Slightly different from the first, but it also looked amazing. We also sold that one quickly.

My amazing friend from work contacted me and asked if I had tried doing image transfers onto wood and if so, could I make her a Japanese-themed clock? I said I would give it a try to see how it went. She had an exact vision of what she wanted which was great.

It worked so well. I was able to transfer the image of a cherry blossom onto the face of the clock and burn Japanese numbers into the face. I was so proud of it, and she loved it so much. I was so excited to drop it off to her. It was everything she wanted.

We started making tables from old scaffold boards with modern metal legs. They were selling so fast. We were onto something here. We just lacked time due to working our Monday to Friday jobs.

Chris had decided that he really wanted to try and take this work full-time and make a business out of it. I felt the same way. We decided to create a website and broadcast that we would be going full-time. We signed up for websites and created profiles to be able to find work. Now we just had to hand our notice in at work. We both gave a month's notice. All of a sudden, out of nowhere, Covid appeared. Bad timing!

Luckily, we had a lot of savings and were able to get some materials to build furniture and sell them without having contact with people. The lockdown was announced, and we were unable to go anywhere.

We decided to get creative at home and build a beautiful garden. Some suppliers were still delivering, so we were able to get some things ordered. We started by building a large deck frame at the back of the garden, but instead of using the usual decking, we ripped apart hundreds of pallets and used the wood to create the deck. We knew it wouldn't last forever, but it looked beautiful once we oiled it. All the colours of the different woods emerged, and it looked so unique.

We then ripped out the horrible grass that never really grew and replaced it with artificial grass. We created a raised step on one side of the garden using some of the bricks we had left from our kitchen wall, which led to the deck, a water feature on the other side using reclaimed railway sleepers, and created a built-in BBQ to create an outdoor kitchen. We put up a very simple pergola over our deck, which looked great. We then accented the front of the deck, the BBQ kitchen, water feature and the whole pergola with black paint and painted the fencing around the garden black too. It was so beautiful and so relaxing having the water feature there.

The only thing we had left to do was to put in a new patio in front of the grass to replace the horrible yellow ones that came with the house. We found a company that was still delivering, so we ordered some slabs and got laying.

The garden was complete. I had been taking progress pictures and posting them online since the start of our project. We had so many inquiries from people asking if we could come and quote them to work on their garden. Covid for us was a godsend because after lockdown, we could meet people outside at a distance and discuss their plans. We could carry out the work with no contact at all. We ended up working without a single break until the end of that year. It was amazing. It's not how we saw the company going and not the direction we expected, but we thought we could do more of what we wanted once we had a good client base and Covid was out the way.

The year came to a close after a very small Christmas. Chris and I spent the time together as we weren't allowed to visit family. We face-timed mum, who was on her own, which was a shame, but we couldn't risk Covid or being caught. We didn't hear from James. I didn't want to be the one to have to reach out; he's my big brother; surely he should do that every now and again?

We had planned the start of our year and had a job waiting for us starting in January. It felt good to go back to work and be busy. We were gaining so much new work through word of mouth that we were booking up to the end of the year already.

It wasn't long until we heard from James. He wasn't looking to catch up; he wanted us to do some work for him. Chris was against it because he thought we would only hear from him when he wanted something, but I suggested we do it to possibly open up an avenue again. Chris was worried I was going to get my heart broken, but he could see how much I wanted to try.

We did some tiling for James in his kitchen. We got on fine, as if nothing had ever happened. It was that whole sweeping under the carpet attitude, which I hated so much. Maybe Chris had been right; maybe this was a mistake.

James threw out an invitation 'someday soon,' to have some drinks together. I knew this would never materialise, so I told him to let me know when they were free. Of course, that time never came.

Since Chris and I couldn't go on holiday that year, we decided that we would look at maybe getting the dogs we always wanted. Chris always wanted a Rottweiler, and I always wanted a brown Doberman. They were the dream dogs that we had talked about for years, and now with our own business and the ability to manage our own time, it felt like now was right. I started to research the breeds and where we could get them from. We found both puppies who were 13 days apart in age and were ready to look for homes. We had picked out our names already before we even had them. The Rottweiler would be called Thor, and the Doberman would be called Loki. Thor was going to come over from Ireland, so we saw him on facetime and spoke to the breeder a great deal. He was so beautiful. Loki was in Birmingham, and we would go and pick him up after Thor had arrived with us. He looked like he was a little terror, but so beautiful.

When Thor arrived with us, I thought my heart would burst. He was just the most perfect, fluffy little guy. He was quite brave and loved the attention he was getting. He was so well-behaved too. The first night he cried a bit but settled quite quickly. Once he had his little brother with him, he would be okay.

The following weekend we went to collect Loki from Birmingham. Of course, we took Thor with us, so he wasn't left at home. I couldn't believe I was about to bring my dream dog home. I went in to get him and paid the remainder of what I owed, and we set off home with my little bundle of joy. It was hard to imagine that something so small was going to turn into something so large. He looked a bit like Arlo the Dinosaur; very cute with huge eyes, but terrified of everything.

When we got them home, we properly introduced the boys. It was so funny. They didn't know what to make of each other, but all Loki wanted to do was cuddle with Thor or just sit on him. Thor was a little growler, though, and was having none of it. We knew then that Thor would always be alpha. They would end up being the best of friends and completely inseparable.

The boys settled, and I feel like they gave us purpose outside of work. They gave us a reason to go out for walks and be in the fresh air, which I feel we neglected. Working outside is very different from a nice walk in the woods.

Work continued to pile in, and we got to the point where we were earning too much money. Worse problems to have! We spoke to our accountant about having to go VAT registered. We didn't want to do this at all because it was so much more administrative work to do, and we would have to add 20% to all our labour costs. We were worried this would put clients off. We had to contact all the clients we had booked in, to tell them that their quote was going to increase. Luckily, all but one client came back and were still happy to proceed, so we continued to work through it.

It wasn't long before things were changing with Covid, and people were allowed to go on holiday again. The reason we had been so successful and completed so many gardens was that people were spending more time at home and were unable to travel. They also had more disposable income available as they weren't traveling. Our workload started to decrease a little, but it was still manageable. We just had to look harder for work.

We decided it would be good for me to go and do a trade course which would help us with the business. Chris was a carpenter, and we thought I could do my own specific trade. I signed up for an electrician's course, which was a fast-track style program. It would mean three weeks of driving to

Brighton every day, but I was excited that I could help extend our services within the business.

I started the course and soon realized how much hard work it was. There were so many maths equations to work through to make sure you were choosing the correct cable and so on. I did, however, finish the course and pass it with flying colours. We could now add some small electrical jobs to our portfolio. I would need to gain experience working with a qualified electrician to work towards taking on bigger, more complicated jobs.

We added small jobs to our projects which gave us an additional boost in earnings. I felt so much more confident that I was doing my bit to help Chris.

Things were really looking up. There was no drama because we really kept family at arm's length, and we concentrated on our own lives.

Chapter 7

'A single word even may be a spark of inextinguishable thought.'

– Percy Shelly

We met with some friends who we hadn't seen since before Covid. We had some drinks and a much-needed catch-up. It was amazing that even though we hadn't seen each other for such a long time, there wasn't much to talk about because no one had been anywhere or done anything. They mentioned that one of their friends was taking their business abroad and leaving the UK. This instantly sparked something in us both, but we didn't really discuss it further.

Chris and I remained busy with work but started to feel restless. Although the business was running well and we were always at capacity, we were now stuck completing garden projects which was not where we saw ourselves going. We wanted to build bespoke furniture and items using reclaimed materials and we felt that we were working so much that we weren't really living. This wasn't what we planned when we started the business.

We felt like we wanted more from life. We had done well; we owned a house, we ran our own successful business, and we had our beautiful boys, who we loved so much. We both were convinced there was more for us. We thought back to the conversation we had with our friends over drinks and threw around the idea of moving abroad. Both of us had thought of Australia, but my heart was in Canada from the trip we had when I was younger. We decided to do some research to see what would be possible.

Australia, although an amazing country, was going to prove hard to get out there and stay there. We were also worried about global warming, and the country warming up further causing more bush fires. The other issue we had was taking the boys with us. Of course, they were coming with us wherever we went, but we needed to make it as stress-free for them as possible. If we decided on Australia, we would have to put them on a minimum of a 24-hour flight to be quarantined on the other side of the country from where we were planning to go. They would have to stay in quarantine for ten days before making their way to us, which could take another week. This was too much and would be so unfair. We decided that this was not the place for us and looked at options in Canada.

As far as the dogs were concerned, with Canada, we could put the dogs on our flight, as long the plane had all the facilities for it and pick them up when we arrive in the country. They had no quarantine, and it was a much shorter flight. This was looking like it could be an option, and we instantly felt rejuvenated and that we had something to work towards. We looked into avenues to get out there and got stuck into researching.

Mum had invited us around for lunch now that we were allowed to visit. I thought I should tell her that we had been looking at the possibility of leaving the UK, but I knew that this would go down like a lead balloon.

I told Chris that I knew the news would not be received well, but he reminded me that I needed to do something for myself. How many times had I put myself out for other people? How many times had I accepted people's blame against me when I had done nothing wrong? All I had ever done was to be honest and reveal the truth. Maybe people don't want to see the truth. I can't live like that. Chris reminded me of how strong I could be and to tell mum that this is what we wanted to do for us.

We sat down and had some drinks whilst mum finished preparing lunch. I looked at Chris, and he could see I was nervous. We caught up on the news and how work had been. It was the usual small talk, but I couldn't really concentrate because I had this other news to tell her. At that time, it was just an idea that needed so much research and work, but I needed to tell her sooner rather than later.

Mum could tell something was going on. I think she was expecting me to tell her I was pregnant, or something that she would actually like to hear. She could never understand that I didn't want children. I looked at Chris in such a way, and he knew he was going to have to take the lead with this one.

Chris told her that we might have an opportunity to move to Canada. Her face dropped, and instantly tears appeared in her eyes. She looked down and turned away to stir the gravy without saying a word. There it was, that guilty feeling back again. I should be used to that feeling by now

She pulled herself together and started asking questions about it, but I could tell she was immediately against the idea. She threw as much negativity toward us as possible to try and put us off. I couldn't understand why people can't be supportive instead of angry about how it might affect them. Why would anyone want to live in the same country their whole lives. There's a whole world out there to explore. She didn't understand at all.

The rest of the day at mum's was somewhat awkward, and I could tell she was cross with me. I knew this was going to happen. I knew she would make it hard for me. The thing that upset me the most was that I had been through so much with Him and had to take so much anger and abuse and allow people to put their blame on me for everything He had done. Why could she not understand that I wanted to go and live a life for myself and put everything behind me for good.

We left mum's, and I sat quietly in the car. Chris patiently waited for me to say something because he could see I was upset. He eventually asked me what it was that I wanted. What did I want for my future? We both wanted the same thing, a clean slate, a fresh start, and we wanted to build our own house in an amazing country.

That week, I decided to text James because he never answered the phone to me. I told him that I wanted to speak to him about our plan, but it seemed mum had told him before I could. He made it very clear that he thought I was being selfish and that I hadn't thought of anyone but myself, but to do what I felt I needed to do. I did find it amusing because many years ago, James had said that he had considered going to live in Dubai to work, and I was nothing but supportive. He decided not to go, and I can only put it down to fear of risk.

'The risk is worth taking if it's going to give you a life worth living.'

- Steven Aitchison.

I had never really forgiven James for his selfishness years ago when I needed him. He couldn't give me an hour of his time to come and sit with me to speak to mum. He was more interested in his football than coming to help me on one of the most difficult days of my life. I have never told him this, and I probably never will because I am not one to try and intentionally make someone feel bad. I will never forget that he didn't come and help me when I needed him though.

We were going to make this work, and it would be a fresh start for us and a chance to get away from negativity and stressors in our lives. We decided to put our house up for sale because the market was so good and we could get a great return. We had an open house and about nine viewings. We ended up having three offers and were able to secure a very good price for our house. We were so excited. The first big step towards our goal.

Around the same time, mum asked what Chris and I were doing for Christmas. I told her that because the house was basically sold, we didn't know where we would be and couldn't really plan anything. She told me that James had invited her to spend Christmas with them, and maybe we could go to hers on Boxing Day to have the day together. I remember thinking that this could potentially be the last Christmas we have in the UK if everything goes to plan, and James still couldn't invite us over for Christmas. We booked a restaurant for our Christmas lunch and were really looking forward to a stress-free time, just the two of us.

In the coming weeks, we decided to step up the research. We gave ourselves a timeline of 18 months. We looked at the best and quickest avenues we could take to get to Canada, and discovered that I could do a course to convert my electrician's qualification and acquire more knowledge. The course would be a year, which would allow us one-year study permit and one-year working permit afterward. During this time, Chris could work as a carpenter. All the houses in Canada are timber frame buildings, so they are always crying out for more carpenters. During our stay in the country, we could apply for permanent residency through specific avenues. There was a huge amount to consider, but we wanted to make it happen. If you really want to make something work, you will.

I wanted Chris to be sure that it was the right place for him and that he would love it as much as I did. We planned to take a trip to Nova Scotia, where the best college was. We could buy an amazing plot of land there for very little money with the aim of building an off-grid home. It was so exciting. We had been researching living off-grid for years and how we could make it work. We wanted to be completely mortgage and bill free and live our lives the way we wanted. We would have solar panels for our power which would include underfloor heating and lighting, but we would also have a wood burner for additional heating in the winter. We would dig a well and add a septic tank. We wanted to do more research on our trip and look at plots of land for sale. We were so excited.

Now that the house was sold, we decided to sell some of our furniture to get the big things out of the way. Our dining table was a huge butcher's block table with ten beautiful oak and leather chairs, but we struggled to find a buyer for it. Finally, we met a couple who were renovating their house and had a lovely big dining room. They came to look at the table and made a deal with us. They would pick it up after our trip, so I took all the listings down as agreed. This was a weight lifted as we didn't want to give it away and taking it with us was out of the question due to size and weight.

We planned our trip to Nova Scotia just after mums 70th birthday so that we could attend her party. Afterall, she was already disappointed that we were going and made us very aware of it at any opportunity. We also agreed to help her organise the catering for the party, so we ordered and collected all of the food for her.

Mum had about fifty guests at her party. She had family friends, and even friends from when James and I were babies. She had a great band playing, and it was a fun evening. Chris and I received a barrage of questions from all of mum's friends about our plan to emigrate. It seemed mum had told everyone about it. I found it difficult to read some people's reactions to it, but a few of them said that we should go for it. If we didn't do it now, we never would.

Chris took some time to pull my brother aside to talk to him about Canada. He told James that he wasn't taking me away; it was a way of life that we wanted. Chris told him that I wanted a relationship with him and not to write us off. It seemed like the conversation went well, but I was soon to learn that it had fallen on deaf ears.

Chapter 8

'Never allow waiting to become a habit. Live your dreams and take risks. Life is happening now.'

– Unknown

The time had come. We were flying out the next day, but first, we had to take the dogs to the kennels we had booked. It seemed like a nice place, as kennels go, but I felt so awful about leaving them there. They had never been away from us in two years, so this was going to be hard for them. We had found somewhere where they could be in the same kennel together so they would at least have each other.

When it came to dropping them off, I was so emotional. It was such a quick process of handing them to the girls and watching them walk off. I didn't realize it was going to be like that. I didn't know I couldn't have one last cuddle. Looking back, it makes sense because the boys would have fed off my emotions and been worried. It didn't stop me from crying when we got back in the car, though. I felt like a big piece of me had just been taken away. They were our babies, and we loved them so much. It was hard to be excited at that moment for our flight in the morning because my emotions were running so high.

We got home and started to get the rest of our things together for our early start in the morning. We would need to leave at five AM to get to the airport. It would be a long day.

We began our trip to Nova Scotia. We first had to get a six-hour flight to Halifax and then drive for around three and a half hours to get to Yarmouth. We were lucky that our flight arrived around an hour early, which shortened our day. As soon as we got into the airport and presented our passports to be inspected, we realized just how friendly people were. The man was amazed that we had the same birthdays and talked to us about our flight and our plans. He couldn't have been nicer. It made a huge change to what we were used to in the UK. I think the English can come across as being very rude and abrupt, so it was a nice welcome.

We had to hire a car for the road trip, so we went to the nearest car rental desk where again, a lovely lady helped us by providing us with a beautiful car for our trip. It was an enormous Ford Explorer, but since we were used to driving a Ford SUV it felt familiar, apart from diving on the other side of the road. That, it seemed, would take some getting used to.

We set off on our road trip. It was so foggy when we arrived, so it was a hazy trip down to Yarmouth, but beautiful, nonetheless. The trip was so easy, with minimal traffic and huge roads surrounded by woodland.

We finally arrived in Yarmouth and checked into our hotel, which was brand new. It was perfect for what we needed on our stay, and again, people couldn't do enough for us.

Although we were only in Yarmouth for five days, we had a lot packed in. On our second day, we visited the college to gather information about the course and made sure that I had everything required to apply. The faculty at the college was so helpful. They gave us so much information and contacts to go away with. The visit was well worthwhile, and I applied for my course for September 2023.

The following day we paid a visit to the realtor we had been speaking to regarding plots of land for sale. She showed us a great app to use, which showed all the properties for sale in Nova Scotia and we could use the mapping system to see exactly how big the plots were when we got to them. We set out to go and find the plots and get an idea of what was around.

We found two beautiful plots on the same road. They were on a stunning little cove, so we would have a sea view and absolute peace and quiet on a two-acre plot. These were the ones. We would have to wait for the sale of our house to go through and get the money ready to buy one of them, but we both felt that this was exactly what we wanted.

For the rest of our trip, we decided to look at some of the local shops, visit some of the beaches, and find the best place to look at the stars. We went to the stunning Cape Forchu lighthouse, where we watched the moon dip into the sea and saw some of the brightest stars either of us had ever seen. It was so beautiful, and we knew we were making the right decision.

Sadly, our trip was coming to an end as we were only there for five days. We had decided to make our drive back to Halifax a day early, so that we wouldn't have to drive early in the morning before our flight.

We stayed in a hotel close to the airport, but Halifax was not like Yarmouth. Being a city, it was busy and congested, the people were not as friendly at all, and we were glad to only be there one night. By now, I was looking forward to getting home and picking up our pups.

We flew home the following day and arrived exhausted. I noticed that I had a voicemail on my phone. I listened to it, and it was a message from our estate agent asking me to give him a call. My heart sank. I knew it was an issue with the sale of our house. I couldn't call him until the following day because it was so late. As I had feared, our agent informed us the next day that our house buyer had dropped out for no reason other than no longer being interested. I was devastated because we would have completed the sale at the start of December, which would mean we could secure our plot of land. There was no other option than to relist the house for sale. Unfortunately, the market had dropped considerably, and interest rates had risen. This was not the best time to sell. We put the house back on the market for the same guide price and waited for viewings to come in.

To make things worse, the couple who were going to buy our dining table also pulled out. We couldn't believe our luck. I relisted the table back on numerous platforms to try and resell it. That same day, I had a message from a lady who wanted to come and see it that same evening. She fell in love with it and took it for £250 more than we were previously going to make. You know what they say, everything happens for a reason.

Whilst being out in Nova Scotia, our realtor informed us that there was a new law coming in January 2023. This was a property prohibition which would mean any non-residents of Canada would be unable to buy land or property. Our realtor said that Yarmouth may be exempt but she would let us know. I was hoping to have one of the plots secured by the end of the year to make sure we avoided the prohibition, but this would no longer be an option. Our fate was in the hands of the Canadian Government. What would be would be.

The phone started ringing with new viewings on our house, and we had lots of people lining up to come and view it. We were feeling a little more optimistic about it and got the house ready. Finally, we had numerous people willing to make an offer, and we accepted at one the guide price. It was a fair bit less than the previous sale, but still a great price. Things were on the up again.

Just as everything was taking a turn for the better, I had a phone call from James. He started asking how everything was going with our plans, about Canada and when we were looking at going. I told him all about it, thinking that maybe the chat that Chris had with him at mum's party had made a difference.

It was then that the line, 'The reason I'm calling…' came out. My heart sank a bit, and I instantly felt angry that he had pretended to be interested in our news just to ask me for a favour. 'Go on,' I said.

He asked if there was a possibility of mum coming to us at Christmas because they had decided to see his wife's family instead. I was so angry. I told him that mum would be upset that they were palming her off. He told me that if we could add another seat to our table at the restaurant, it would be a great help. 'I'll see what I can do,' I told him.

The restaurant couldn't accommodate another chair for the time we were eating, so I let James know via text and waited for his response. We were eating at 3:00pm because we had made plans in the morning to walk the dogs with friends and have a late lunch to give us time to get ready.

A few days later, very late in the evening, I got a text from James. He said, 'I hope you don't mind, but we phoned the restaurant to see when they could have three people come for lunch on Christmas Day, and they can do 12:15'. They did what?? 12:15 was never going to work for us because of our plans. My blood was boiling; I felt sick that they would actually check what time we could change our lunch to accommodate their change of plans. Who does that?!

While James was texting me, Chris received an email from the restaurant about the booking we had made, saying that they had spoken to Mrs. Hickman and that our booking had been changed to 12:15. Not only had they phoned up to see when we could eat, they pretended to be us and requested to change our booking!! By this point, I felt numb. I thought there was no end to the lies and narcissism in my family. I sat there speechless while Chris was swearing, furious about how rude they were.

I texted James, saying that he was completely out of line and that he expected us to change our plans so that they could change theirs. He had been the one to invite mum in the first place, and now he had changed his mind. I told him that mum was going to be upset about it. He didn't plan on telling her; he was relying on me to tell her. Down to me to break the news to her again then; this all felt so familiar. Chris and I said to each other, 'Just another reason.' This meant just another reason to have a fresh start in Canada and live our own lives the way we want.

We both had a sleepless night because we were so enraged and completely astonished at the nerve of my brother. I often wonder if the people that cause this kind of rage sleep at night.

I woke up in the morning to find that Chris had sent them a message in anger, saying that we would not be changing our plans for them. This fuelled my rage because I had asked him to stay out of it. I could understand why he had done it, but overnight, I had decided that we could cancel the restaurant and have mum over for dinner instead because I wanted to make sure she would be ok. I told him that I was annoyed that he had done that without me knowing. He apologised, saying that he was just so angry that whenever they clicked their fingers, everyone had to jump. He was, of course correct, but he hadn't helped the situation. I could see he felt bad, but I said to him, this is our last Christmas here, and to think of our end goal.

I responded to the message saying that we would invite mum for the day, but she would be upset about it. She always felt second best to the rest James' family. James responded by saying that I hadn't considered mum at all, which was grossly unfair. We hadn't considered anyone because we didn't know where we would be living, and we had been very honest about it from the start. I could only assume he was also referring to our upcoming move to Canada. He had upset me so much, and I was in floods of tears. I wondered what he was turning into as a person and the way he thought that it was acceptable to treat people.

I called mum, feeling like my heart was in my throat. I knew that I was going to cry, but I really didn't want to because I didn't want mum to feel like it was a chore for us to have her over for Christmas Day. She answered, and I asked her if she wouldn't mind coming to us for Christmas. My voice was trembling a bit as I was struggling to hold back my emotions. She told me that she was supposed to be with James. That's when I explained what had happened, and I broke. I was a mess. I was still appalled at what they had done and how they had pretended to be us to change our dinner booking. Mum was as shocked as we were and actually quite disgusted.

I tried to explain to her that I wasn't upset about the fact that she was coming to us for Christmas; it was the way James had treated me and how he had gone about things. I also told her that I felt bad for her because they had found it so easy to palm her off and be with his other family. As predicted, she was upset. She was upset that it was them over her again. I told her to express her feelings to James, but she never did. This is exactly why issues in my family will never be resolved, and I will always be blamed. I am the only one who tells people the truth, and they hate it! Why are people so afraid of the truth?

So, here we are. It was at that moment, I decided to write this book, because I was fed up with being the one who everyone blamed; with being chosen second after Him. He destroyed everything with His social habits, with His gambling problems, He who took out a ridiculous mortgage which almost completely destroyed my mum's life. After all this, my family gives Him their time; they give Him more time than me which I just don't understand and never will.

I thought writing this book would give me clarity as to why my family behaves the way they do. Honestly, I still can't understand it; I still can't see the logic. The most important thing for us now is to reach our goal for 2023 and make our move to Canada to live the way we want to live. I need the negativity and blame out of my life and to concentrate on living, not regretting. So, here's to our next chapter!

Chapter 9

'The simplest questions are the hardest to answer.'

– Northrop Frye

<u>Do I wish I had never found it?</u>

I wish I had never found it at such a young age. I wish I had been old enough to understand it all properly.

<u>Would I change it?</u>

No, I wouldn't. It taught me a lot about truth and honesty and how important it is regardless of the consequences.

<u>Do I wish I didn't know what I know now?</u>

Absolutely not. I am glad I know who He is, and I'm glad I know who my family are. I also know who I am and honestly I am proud of myself. Although it has been heart breaking, and revealing, I would rather know. The truth shall set you free, and as long as you accept it and don't dwell on it, you can move past it.

<u>Should I have said anything?</u>

I still believe I was right to tell mum everything. Even if she didn't actually want to know and would have quite happily swept everything under the carpet, I know I was right. Always own your decisions, and don't let people tell you differently. Don't regret your decisions because they shape you.

Does counselling help?

Absolutely. It doesn't matter if you use it just to get everything off your plate to an impartial person or to use it to learn how to deal with your situation. I used it for both. I still use the exercises now and look to find a positive in any situation. Ultimately, it has made me a stronger, more positive person.

Does everyone blame me?

I don't think mum blames me. I feel there is resentment there but also pity. I hate the pity. My brother absolutely blames me for all of it. If it makes him feel better to blame me, then I will take that burden, but I won't have a relationship with him.

How the hell have they forgiven him?

This, I will never know and never understand. I am the kind of person who will write people off for wronging me. I won't give my time to those I can't trust. Life is too short to spend time with people you don't truly know. I have a small circle of friends around me who I love and trust, and my amazing husband who knows all my worst bits, and it's ok.

How could they spend time with Him and not me?

I can't imagine why they would want to see Him. I never want to see Him again. But to choose Him over me is definitely an unknown entity and can't be explained other than blame and resentment.

Should I resent them for seeing Him?

I shouldn't, but I do. I think it is a natural reaction. I blocked images on social media because they stirred up too many emotions of resentment and confusion. It makes my blood boil every time mum says she has seen Him, but it's her choice, so I have to reel in my rage.

Where would we all be now if I hadn't said anything?

Who knows. Maybe I would have a relationship with James, but my mum would potentially be in the same situation after the debt, the mortgage, and the house sale. The family would still be split, and mum would still be divorced. It's just a pity about my relationship with my brother. With this in mind, the family split would be inevitable and this then takes the responsibility away from me and means I shouldn't carry guilt for this, but I still do.

Does this get easier?

I think it does get better because it gets easier. For me, separating myself and distancing was key to a more positive outlook. Also, having the love, support, and complete understanding of my husband and closest friends has been life-changing for me.

Has it made me a different person, and would I be who I am today if it had never happened?

I am a different person. Looking at it through my positive mindset it's made me stronger and more resilient. On the flip side, it has made me suspicious of people and much less trusting, but with the way people treat each other these days, maybe it's not a bad thing. I keep a small circle of friends who I absolutely trust and love. I am wary about letting new people in but given time I can learn to trust.

Is it better to run from it all and accept that everyone blames me?

Although some say I am running, I would disagree. I am finally on the road to living a life I love with my incredible husband and our beautiful dogs. We aim to live mortgage and bill free in a beautiful country. I accept that James blaming me makes it easier for him, which is sad, but maybe one day, he will realize that it's not my fault. I think both mum and James resent me and think I am partially responsible for the split in the family and the frayed relationships. I will never be able to change their opinion of me, so I will no longer try. My time is now.

Am I that selfish person that they think I am?

I'm not selfish, quite the opposite in fact. As far as I'm concerned, I told everyone what they needed me to know. If I was in a situation like mum, I would absolutely want to know. I guess the truth really does hurt; it just doesn't hurt the way you think it will.

'If you don't leave your past in the past, it will destroy your future. Live for what today has to offer, not what yesterday has taken away.'

- Unknown

CPSIA information can be obtained
at www.ICGtesting.com
Printed in the USA
LVHW052050230123
737778LV00012B/1349